New Directions for
Institutional Research

Robert K. Toutkoushian
EDITOR-IN-CHIEF

J. Fredericks Volkwein
ASSOCIATE EDITOR

Workforce Development and Higher Education

A Strategic Role for Institutional Research

Richard A. Voorhees
Lee Harvey
EDITORS

Number 128 • Winter 2005
Jossey-Bass
San Francisco

WORKFORCE DEVELOPMENT AND HIGHER EDUCATION: A STRATEGIC ROLE FOR
INSTITUTIONAL RESEARCH
Richard A. Voorhees, Lee Harvey (eds.)
New Directions for Institutional Research, no. 128
Robert K. Toutkoushian, Editor-in-Chief

Copyright © 2005 Wiley Periodicals, Inc., A Wiley Company

NEW DIRECTIONS FOR INSTITUTIONAL RESEARCH (ISSN 0271-0579, electronic
ISSN 1536-075X) is part of The Jossey-Bass Higher and Adult Education
Series and is published quarterly by Wiley Subscription Services, Inc., A
Wiley Company, at Jossey-Bass, 989 Market Street, San Francisco, California 94103-1741 (publication number USPS 098-830). Periodicals
Postage Paid at San Francisco, California, and at additional mailing
offices. POSTMASTER: Send address changes to New Directions for Institutional Research, Jossey-Bass, 989 Market Street, San Francisco, California 94103-1741.

SUBSCRIPTIONS cost $80.00 for individuals and $170.00 for institutions,
agencies, and libraries. See order form at end of book.

EDITORIAL CORRESPONDENCE should be sent to Robert K. Toutkoushian,
Educational Leadership and Policy Studies, Education 4220, 201 N. Rose
Ave., Indiana University, Bloomington, IN 47405.

New Directions for Institutional Research is indexed in *College Student
Personnel Abstracts, Contents Pages in Education,* and *Current Index to Jour-
nals in Education* (ERIC).

Microfilm copies of issues and chapters are available in 16mm and 35mm,
as well as microfiche in 105mm, through University Microfilms Inc., 300
North Zeeb Road, Ann Arbor, Michigan 48106-1346.

www.josseybass.com

CONTENTS

EDITORS' NOTES

This volume of *New Directions for Institutional Research* originated at a joint
symposium on workforce development cosponsored by the European Association for Institutional Research (EAIR) and the Association for Institutional
Research (AIR), held in Amsterdam in June 2003. The Amsterdam symposium was a first effort to create a series of scholarly meetings between these
two professional associations and was devoted to a single topic of interest. It
attracted an alert audience of practitioners and scholars from throughout
Europe, America, Canada, Asia, and Australia. The range of participant experiences both outside and within higher education made for energetic debate
and an interchange of new ideas about higher education's role in preparing
students for work. Attendees left with new perspectives on how higher education can deal with what governments increasingly expect in return for
financial support of institutions: an educated and skilled citizenry that can
contribute to economic growth in a progressively global economy.

The goal of this volume is to build on that symposium by giving institutional research personnel an understanding of the nature of workforce
development, especially as it applies to Europe and the United States. As
symposium attendees learned, the concept of workforce development does
not carry the same meaning on both sides of the Atlantic. Even though all
agreed that the connections between workforce development and higher
education were fundamental, the cultural, institutional, and government
philosophies vary markedly around the globe. The role of institutional
research in dealing with workforce development also depends on context.
For example, the job category "institutional researcher" is virtually unknown in Europe; those engaged in what might be described in the United
States as institutional research are typically embedded in academic areas
within a college or university and not centralized in a single office serving
the entire institution, as is typical in North American institutions. In contrast, EAIR members are usually engaged in policy work on behalf of their
employers, not in day-to-day research and data analysis to support institutional operations and management.

The first of the eight chapters in this volume, written by Richard A.
Voorhees and Lee Harvey, explores the strategic role that institutional
research offices can play in helping their institutions evaluate strategies for
meeting workforce needs in their states and nations. Chapter Two, contributed by Harvey and titled "Embedding and Integrating Employability,"
reviews efforts institutions have made to define the skills and competencies
necessary in the workforce. Harvey traces the need to work with employers
adequately so that they understand the types of employee they require at a
time when the value of a degree is under question. Similarly, he addresses

NEW DIRECTIONS FOR INSTITUTIONAL RESEARCH, no. 128, Winter 2005 © Lee Harvey. Printed with permission.

the development of employment-related attributes by institutions. Drawing from exemplary institutions in the United Kingdom and elsewhere, this chapter considers the future of these efforts, which have received increasing attention over the past decade.

Chapter Three, "Using Research to Align Programs," also by Voorhees, presents techniques that institutional researchers can use to judge the market potential for new programs and to refine existing programs. As the needs of the labor market change, institutions must adapt. Portions of this article first appeared in *NDIR* number 54, "Designing and Using Market Research" (edited by Robert S. Lay and Jean J. Endo) in 1988. Almost two decades later, changing methodologies and techniques driven chiefly by data and information now quickly found on the Internet have made it easier than ever to harvest profiles of prospective students, employment, and industry-specific data. Even so, how can institutions use this information to their best advantage when aligning their programs? What are the pitfalls in assessing the employment market for graduates?

Chapter Four, by Mantz Yorke and Lee Harvey, is titled "Graduate Attributes and Their Development"; it explores the skills that higher education must impart if graduates are to succeed in the workplace. The authors report convergence among employers on the skills that are desired of new employees and on these skills not always being subject-specific. Adaptability, flexibility, and willingness to learn are the skills of graduates that the labor market seeks most. The authors present a theoretical model for practitioners to understand the elements of employability and the apportioning of responsibility for students obtaining employment.

Chapter Five, "Accountability Measures in Workforce Training" by Kent Phillippe, examines the current status of reporting outcome and other data to government agencies. Within the United States, Phillippe examines the reporting burden brought about by the Carl D. Perkins Vocational-Technical Education Act (commonly referred to as Perkins III) and the Workforce Investment Act (WIA) and suggests prototypical models that promote nimble institutional response to labor market realities while meeting the legitimate needs of funding agencies. Phillippe notes that certain governments in Europe appear to be heading toward decentralization of accountability at a time when the United States is moving in the opposite direction. At the same time, quality assurance techniques are needed by all providers of workforce training to ensure that programs embark on a path to continuous improvement.

Chapter Six, by Sven Junghagen of the Graduate School of Business at Copenhagen Business School, examines the connections between curriculum development and graduate employability in a European setting. He presents a blueprint for engaging academicians in the process of aligning what is taught with what is required by employers. Techniques for validating an institutional qualifications framework, including systematic communication strategies with business and industry, are offered.

Chapter Seven focuses on enabling economically disadvantaged students to enter higher education, a feature of what is termed in parts of Europe as "widening participation." Julian L. Alssid and his colleagues explore the development of career pathway models in the United States that aim to build bridges for disadvantaged adults into further and higher education and thus to economic self-sufficiency. These career pathway approaches seek to ensure that participants are prepared for the labor market. Although apparatus in the United States tends to be different from that in most European countries, the underlying philosophy espoused in this chapter is well suited to the European situation.

Chapter Eight, "An Action Agenda for Institutional Researchers," by Harvey and Voorhees, concludes this volume by sketching the various ways in which institutional researchers can become more involved in institutional activities related to employability and workforce development. It suggests that far from being just data collectors, workforce development offers institutional researchers the opportunity to work more closely with other internal and external stakeholders and to have an impact on strategy, policy, and practices designed to enhance student employability and position their institutions accordingly. Unless key institutional partners are brought into the process, techniques and the data they produce may be useless at a time when hearts and minds can be won.

Richard A. Voorhees
Lee Harvey
Editors

RICHARD A. VOORHEES is principal of Voorhees Group LLC, an independent higher education consulting company in Littleton, Colorado.

LEE HARVEY is professor and director of the Centre for Research and Evaluation at Sheffield Hallam University, United Kingdom.

1

*This chapter discusses how workforce development
initiatives vary widely across governments and
institutions, and how institutional research can help
bridge the gaps between them.*

Higher Education and Workforce Development: A Strategic Role for Institutional Research

Richard A. Voorhees, Lee Harvey

As was mentioned in the Editors' Notes, this volume is a by-product of the joint symposium on workforce development cosponsored by the European Association for Institutional Research (EAIR) and the Association for Institutional Research (AIR). Among the first issues to be resolved by participants were the numerous differences in terminology used around the world for describing institutional research and workforce issues. Several terms, although well worn among some participants, were new to others. Terms that were new to symposium participants from the United States included *employability, qualifications*, and *national qualification frameworks*. Employability refers to the capacity of an individual to get a job and the ability to retain it. For the individual, employability depends on the knowledge, skills, and attitudes he or she has and how those assets are used and presented to employers. The burden of employability, then, resides foremost with the graduate's individual attributes and to a lesser degree with the institution. In European colleges and universities, employability refers more to a general set of skills of value to employers and less to ensuring that students leave an institution with a narrow skill set associated with a particular job. In contrast, at least within institutions focused on workforce development, the focus tends to be on specific skills needed for specific jobs.

Qualifications are analogous to what Americans call a degree or certificate. However, in a non-American context a qualification also recognizes that a person has achieved learning outcomes or competencies relevant to identified individual, professional, industry, or community needs. The

NEW DIRECTIONS FOR INSTITUTIONAL RESEARCH, no. 128, Winter 2005 © Lee Harvey. Printed with permission.

match between these competencies and a formal award is the bedrock of a national qualification system and serves higher education in these countries as a mechanism for evaluating institutional quality. Although regional accrediting agencies in the United States have moved in this general direction, qualification systems in the United Kingdom, Australia, and Denmark are further along in specifying and measuring competencies as the sine qua non of higher education. Having said that, academia in these countries is coy about referring to competencies, or even skills, and prefers to frame the development of generic skills in a holistic way, linking them to "higher-level" academic skill development. The preferred terminology for graduate abilities is either the triad "knowledge, skills, and attitudes" or the shorter "attributes."

In developing their own qualification system, many countries have invested heavily in describing not only what holders of those qualifications should be able to demonstrate but also the existing relationships among awards conferred by different levels of education. Two efforts mark progress in the United States toward creating universal competency frameworks. The first is the Secretary's Commission on Achieving Necessary Skills (SCANS), a project that is now more than a decade old and less academic than vocational in scope. The second is ONET, an online system developed by the U.S. Department of Labor's Employment and Training Administration, which at one level seeks to categorize jobs according to competencies and skills.

Other differences mark the approaches to workforce development in Europe and the United States. Centralization of government strategy is the distinguishing factor. American higher education has not been centralized at the national level, although some would argue that it is now moving in that direction.[1] Instead, state governments oversee fifty systems of higher education. European higher education governance, in contrast, flows predominantly from national governments that not only approve establishment of new institutions, departments, and programs but also control the size of enrollment, tuition rate, required courses, minimum graduation credits, and other factors at publicly supported institutions. It is beyond the scope of this volume to explicate fully the differences between centralized and decentralized systems of higher education, except to note that a coordinated national strategy for workforce development that seeks to engage higher education is more difficult to approach when governance is fragmented.

European nations have also committed to increasing participation in higher education. Expansion of these opportunities was the byword of the 1990s, a decade that culminated in the Bologna Declaration. Among other issues to which twenty-nine European higher education ministers committed their governments in Bologna was creation of a "European Higher Education Area" by 2010, to be populated by three common degree cycles: bachelor's, master's, and Ph.D. degrees. The first-cycle degree, the bachelor's, was established as a minimum three-year degree to be relevant to the

European labor market. Prior to Bologna, the bachelor's degree was an academic designation unheard of in many countries in continental Europe. Combined with the mandate that this new degree be connected to labor needs, its introduction is creating unprecedented change in higher education in Europe. This sea change, in tandem with the European Commission's steady push for workforce development, was intended to enhance the employability of all graduates, as well as widen the socioeconomic base of those entering higher education.

Workforce Development and Institutions

At the institutional level, engagement in workforce development can drive an institution's mission or simply be a by-product. In the United States, among other missions, most community colleges embrace workforce development. In the United Kingdom, what were polytechnic universities became full-fledged universities over the past decade, a transformation that has had the concomitant effect of spreading the need to engage in workforce development throughout the "older" universities. On both sides of the Atlantic, institutional longevity appears negatively correlated with workforce engagement. The hierarchy of institutional prestige frequently rests on research and the resources it brings an institution. The upper tiers of higher education are more likely to view work-related training as belonging to "lesser" or "vocational" institutions. The attitude that student choice of major or occupation is uncontrollable and hence outside the institution's sphere of influence is also a factor accounting for lack of inertia.

It is no surprise, then, that employability has been embraced, embedded, and developed more quickly in the new universities in the UK than in the older ones. A similar situation has evolved in Germany, Scandinavia, and the Netherlands, where research universities have also been rather slow in addressing employability issues. This distinction is somewhat premature, however, since vocational education is not the same as employability development. It is just as important to develop employability among English literature and sociology graduates as it is among nurses and engineers. Indeed, some of the most vocational of programs (such as medicine) are mainly confined to long-established research universities. These, though, tend to mistakenly assume that the specialized training offered is tantamount to providing employability skills.

Higher education sorts out issues of tradition, culture, and philosophy, but the global workforce is changing profoundly and won't wait for higher education to catch up. The post–World War II baby boom generation has now reached the zenith of its economic contribution. They soon will reach the traditional retirement age of sixty-five and will need to be replaced by younger workers. Coupled with slow population growth in most countries in North America and Europe, a critical shortage of qualified workers is looming. Employers will experience a difficult time in recruiting replacement workers from a smaller pool. Furthermore, the workforce will require additional training to match advances in technology. In the global economy, many jobs, especially in the manufacturing area, have moved to Asia. There will always be room for jobs that require strength, stamina, and dexterity, but high-paying jobs are linked inextricably to high skills. The skilled workforce of the future will require more verbal, mathematical, and human relation skills than previous generations possessed.

A Role for Higher Education

The connections between a country's education system and its skilled workforce are inescapable. This relationship is intensely symbiotic; the supply of educated workers also influences the quality of a country's education system. A high level of participation in training and education creates an even higher level of future participation. In a global economy, those countries and systems of higher education that do not promote avenues to increase their participation rate are greatly disadvantaged. The pace of change dictates that they will never catch up. Around the world, workers without skills will find themselves unemployed during periods of global economic downturn. Although some skills can be learned simply by osmosis, improving the skill set of a large number of workers requires their participation in formal learning.

In the United States, many working adults received their elementary and secondary education during an era when the knowledge and skills required for a good job were not so rigorous as that demanded by in today's environment. Many adults who were adequately prepared for work in earlier decades must now go back to school to find or keep a good job. Advances in technology and global competition are continuously making obsolete the specific skills of even the most educated adults. Sadly, a large number of adults have not been adequately educated. Undereducated adults and their children most frequently live in poverty. Not only do their states and communities bear the costs of social services necessitated by that poverty, they also lose the contributions these adults might make to society (and the tax rolls) if they were better educated. The wide disparity in income that drives the education and work agenda in the United States is not an overriding motivation in Europe, where disparity in income is narrower.

A Role for Institutional Research

It would seem that most of the activities supporting workforce development may be only tangential to an office of institutional research. Institutional researchers usually are not invited to participate in curriculum development at their institution; nor are they typically charged with bringing together businesses and university leaders to discuss strategies in workforce development and training. Yet many of the tasks accomplished under the umbrella of institutional research are exactly what an institution needs to successfully address workforce issues. An aggressive stance taken by institutional research can shape institutional posture. The key intersections are data-intensive forecasting of new programs, estimating the participation rate of adult learners, and assisting an institution to assess its outcomes in workforce development, especially if its activities are monitored by external agencies. But none of this is simple work.

Despite the existence of national data systems in America, it is not simple to trace a direct connection from higher education programs to labor markets. For example, most higher education institutions in the United States are obligated to describe their instructional programs with Classification for Instructional Programs (CIP) codes. On the job side, the Bureau of Labor Statistics of the federal Department of Labor uses the Standard Occupational Classification (SOC) system to classify workers into occupational categories for the purpose of collecting, calculating, or disseminating data. SOC codes are used by another Department of Labor Employment and Training Administration project, the Occupational Information Network (ONET). The ONET database describes more than 950 occupations by skills, abilities, knowledge, tasks, work activities, work context, experience level required, job interests, and work values and needs. Unfortunately, there is no clear one-to-one correspondence between CIP codes and SOC codes by themselves or the ONET system.

The participation rate of adults in formal learning is one measure of higher education's contribution to workforce development and is an area that institutional researchers should heed. To be sure, it is but one index among numerous potential indicators of an institution's contribution to economic well-being. For example, higher education also produces research and development outcomes, an activity that occurs almost exclusively in major research universities. Performance measures for community colleges are also likely to include the percentage of graduates who either enter the labor force or continue their education upon graduation. All higher education institutions aid their local economy through payroll, purchasing of supplies and material, and the taxable income earned by employees. However, the participation of adults aged twenty-five and older is arguably a more visible indicator of the connections an institution may make between workforce and economic development.

In 1999, for example, the National Center for Education Statistics reported that nearly seventy-six million American adults (less than half of all adults) participated in formal learning (the most recent year for which figures are available; Creighton and Hudson, 2002). In Europe there has also been growing emphasis on lifelong learning and on continuous professional development, both of which have led to a broadening of the activities in which higher education institutions engage. Indeed, some European institutions see this as having more potential as a growth area than conventional degree education; this is almost certainly the case among forward-thinking

American institutions. Still, adult enrollment in degree-granting institutions in the United States is about 12 percent of the total market for adult learners, a figure that was relatively flat throughout the last decade (Voorhees and Lingenfelter, 2003). To be certain, higher education is not totally synonymous with adult education. However, there is considerable room at most institutions to better serve adult learners.

But where are the rest of the adult learners? They are enrolled in work-related and nonwork-related instruction provided by a variety of entities ranging from employee-sponsored training programs to programs sponsored by adult education and community groups. The majority of adult learners were attending proprietary vocational education institutions that do not award an associate's degree or beyond, continuing education programs that do not lead to a degree, or courses and programs offered by organizations not eligible to participate in federal financial aid programs. For example, nearly 1.6 million information technology certifications were awarded outside of degree-granting institutions by 1999 (Adelman, 2000). The rise of corporate universities, the popularity of e-learning opportunities, aggressive recruitment on the part of alternative providers, and the evolving willingness of employers to accept alternative credentials have generated more and new kinds of learning opportunity among adults and a substantially better chance of having that learning rewarded. The breadth of these activities points to an insatiable appetite for adult learning. Still, in the United States more than half of all adults—some ninety-four million people—do not participate in any formal learning activity.

If adult participation in higher education is lower than might be expected to elevate the general level of workplace skills, the total participation of adults in workplace learning, regardless of source, is more sobering. Forty million adults are enrolled in some form of work-related formal learning, but the total number of workers numbers more than 140 million (U.S. Department of Labor, 2001). Given the value of work-related training to national economic health, one must ask whether a participation rate in formal work-related learning of less than one-third of all workers is acceptable and what might be possible with even an incremental increase in work-related skills in benefits to workers, their employers, and the national economy.

Institutional researchers can also help their institutions understand the realities of the employment market. The public's perception of the role of higher education in workforce development is undoubtedly more influenced by intuition than by fact. For example, the Bureau of Labor Statistics recently released projections of the fastest-growing occupations in the United States to the year 2012 (Bureau of Labor Statistics, 2004). Of the thirty occupations listed, eleven required a bachelor's degree or higher. The remainder—more than 60 percent of the total—required an associate degree or less. Although most Americans would agree that a bachelor's degree is required for entry into a high-paying occupation, the data indicate that many labor market needs can be substantially met at the associate degree level or lower. In the

UK, access to some occupations is dependent on securing professional status, mediated by professional or regulatory bodies. In many but not all cases, professional status is contingent on having an undergraduate degree, and sometimes a postgraduate qualification.

The 1998 Workforce Investment Act (WIA) marked a watershed in federal policy to train workers in the United States. It sought to coordinate a hodgepodge of federal programs intended to train a skilled workforce while still preserving "local control." Under WIA, higher education is one of the providers of workforce trainers, subject to the approval of a local Workforce Investment Board and regulations and rules adopted by the state. The federal government has had an increasing voice in higher education, primarily through furnishing resources indirectly to institutions via students. WIA carries on this tradition of decentralized decision making. The second prong of federal resources earmarked for workforce development can be found in the Carl D. Perkins Vocational-Technical Education Act, commonly referred to as Perkins III. This law makes resources available to states to allocate to secondary and postsecondary institutions that are engaged in career and technical education. Like WIA, Perkins III promulgates a series of performance measures that are reported to the federal government, marking a watershed in the federal relationship with higher education. Further, these outcome measures have funding consequences for institutions. Accountability factors for both programs are explored in Kent Phillippe's Chapter Five, dealing with accountability.

Note

1. Although the U.S. government does not govern higher education per se, it exercises an increasingly influential role in overall institutional finance, primarily through providing financial aid directly to needy students. As economic theory would have it, financially enabled students can choose which institution to attend. This market model of financial aid comes with a price: the reporting burden that is attendant on receiving authorization to award federal financial aid is often cited as burdensome. At the same time, however, this federal oversight falls far short of the dictates that a centralized bureaucracy might make on institutions.

References

Adelman, C. "A Parallel Postsecondary Universe: The Certification System in Information Technology." Washington, D.C.: U.S. Department of Education, 2000.

Bureau of Labor Statistics. "Fastest Growing Occupations, 2002–2012." Retrieved July 13, 2004, http://www.bls.gov/emp/emptab3.htm. 2004.

Creighton, S., and Hudson, L. (National Center for Education Statistics). *Participation Trends and Patterns in Adult Education: 1991 to 1999.* NCES 2002–119. Washington, D.C.: U.S. Department of Education, U.S. Government Printing Office, 2002.

U.S. Department of Labor. "Labor Force." *Occupational Outlook Quarterly,* 2001, 45(4), 36–41.

Voorhees, R., and Lingenfelter, P. "Adult Learners and State Policy." Denver: State Higher Education Executive Officers, 2003.

RICHARD A. VOORHEES is principal of Voorhees Group LLC, an independent higher education consulting company in Littleton, Colorado.

LEE HARVEY is professor and director of the Centre for Research and Evaluation at Sheffield Hallam University, United Kingdom.

2

Who bears the responsibility for ensuring that graduates are prepared to enter the job market? This chapter explores the issues surrounding the employability of graduates.

Embedding and Integrating Employability

Lee Harvey

In common with worldwide calls to link higher education more closely with workforce development, the United Kingdom has moved ahead rapidly in promoting this interface. It is a major concern of the current government, picking up and developing such initiatives from the 1990s as enterprise in higher education. The National Committee of Inquiry into Higher Education, also known as the Dearing Report, published in 1997, gave further impetus to the development of employability. The ensuing debate is about what employers want and what higher education institutions can do to enhance the employability of students.

Defining Employability

Employability is a contentious concept, with a plethora of microinterpretations (Harvey, 2001; Lees, 2002). The many definitions of employability are variants of the propensity of graduates to secure a job and progress in their career (LTSN Generic Centre, 2003). However, employability is not just about getting a job; it is about developing attributes, techniques, or experience for life. It is about learning, and the emphasis is less on "employ" and more on "ability." In essence, the emphasis is on developing critical reflective abilities, with a view to empowering and enhancing the learner. Employment is a by-product of this enabling process.

The Enhancing Student Employability Co-ordination Team (ESECT) in the UK has defined employability as "a set of achievements, skills, understandings and personal attributes that make graduates more likely to gain

NEW DIRECTIONS FOR INSTITUTIONAL RESEARCH, no. 128, Winter 2005 © Lee Harvey. Printed with permission. 13

employment and be successful in their chosen occupations, which benefits themselves, the workforce, the community and the economy." Three points need to be made regarding this definition:

1. It is probabilistic. There is no certainty that possessing a range of desirable characteristics will convert employability into employment; there are too many extraneous socioeconomic variables for that.

2. The choice of occupation is, for many graduates, likely to be constrained. They may have to accept that their first occupational choice will not be realistic in the prevailing circumstances, and aim instead for another option that calls on the capabilities they have developed.

3. The gaining of a "graduate job" and success in it should not be conflated. Higher education awards describe the graduate's past performance, but some achievements vital for workplace success might not be covered, not least because of the difficulty of measuring characteristics such as drive, cooperative working, and leadership.

The relationships among higher education graduate, institution, and employer are complex and depend on how graduates have engaged with employability development opportunities, including those afforded by institutions as part of the curriculum; institution-based extracurricular activities (such as those offered by central services, or through work experience placements); and activities beyond the boundaries of the institution, whether paid or unpaid work. The pedagogical processes and reflection on and articulation of learning are essential elements that are mediated by subject discipline and external factors, not least the extracurricular experience of graduates and ultimately the recruitment practices of employers.

A key role for institutional researchers in this process is to undertake an audit of the types of opportunity available to students and to analyze take-up, not only the proportion of target groups but also the characteristics of those who make use of voluntary or extracurricular services and also those who capitalize on the embedded employability elements within curricula. Institutional researchers could investigate how current students interact with employer recruitment practices, not least their experience of Web-based recruitment. Institutional researchers might also follow up graduates and alumni to identify what employability development opportunities they used and which have been important in obtaining a job, developing the job, and progressing in their chosen career. The model of graduate employability (Figure 2.1) depicts the interrelationship of these factors.

Employer Views and Recruitment Practices

Studies in the 1990s and earlier showed that although employers considered an undergraduate experience to be beneficial, they doubted its efficacy as a preparation for work (de la Harpe, Radloff, and Wyber, 2000; Medhat,

Figure 2.1. Model of Graduate Employability Development

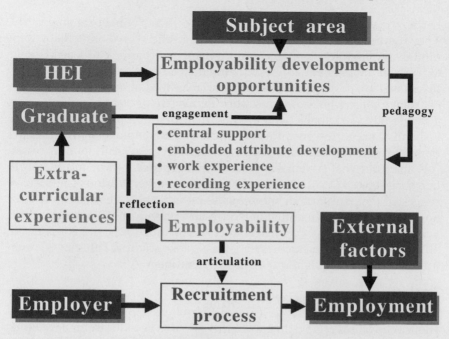

Source: Adapted from Harvey, Locke, and Morey (2002).

2003). Younger, full-time students, other than those who have had a significant placement (internship) experience in their course, often leave university with little idea of the nature and culture of the workplace and find it initially difficult to adjust. This period of adjustment is a cost that graduate employers are no longer able or willing to bear. Thus higher education programs are now expected to better prepare graduates for workplace culture.

Although some employers have entrenched and outdated notions of undergraduate education, others recognize the advances in employability. There is, though, no single employer view across sectors, and indeed often not a single view within an organization. Line managers, graduate recruiters, and strategic managers may express differing expectations of graduates (Johnson, Pere-Vergé, and Hanage, 1993; Cannon, 1986; Mansergh, 1990; Burrows, Harvey, and Green, 1992; Harvey, Moon, and Geall, 1997). Nonetheless, despite premium salaries and reservations about graduates' abilities, employers consider that graduates are cost-effective and that a degree education is beneficial for the graduate as well as adding value to the organization.

Employers' Recruitment Criteria

Employers want recruits who are going to be effective in a changing world. They want people who can deal with change and thrive on it. They want intelligent, flexible, adaptable employees who are quick to learn (this is explored in more detail in Chapter Four). Graduates are much more likely than nongraduates to meet these criteria. In a world of uncertainty, employers want people who are able to work on a range of tasks simultaneously. They do not need people who are resistant to new approaches or slow to respond to cues. However, there is evidence that employers do not always in practice use the best criteria and follow the best recruitment processes. It is important that students appreciate this, especially those most likely to find themselves at a disadvantage in the labor market. Various studies have suggested that recruitment and progression in employment continue to be dogged by bias and inequitable treatment (Harvey and Blackwell, 1999; Egerton, 2001; Blasko, Brennan, Little, and Shah, 2002; CEL, 2002; CIHE, 2002). Institutional researchers could undertake studies of alumni to examine whether there is significant bias in recruitment.

Developments in Higher Education

Higher education establishments in the UK have been active in developing the employability agenda, not only in skills development but in linking it to pedagogy and ensuring that employability is embedded in the curriculum and that there is an integrated approach across the institution (Harvey, Locke, and Morey, 2002). In the late 1990s, skill development was the dominant approach adopted by institutions. However, as analysis of employer needs and graduate attributes became more sophisticated, there has been a shift away from "skills" in a narrow sense of a few specific key skills. The shift in higher education is from attribute development in specialist modules or extracurricular activity to a more holistic approach that embeds employability as part of academic learning.

There are four broad areas of activity that higher education institutions are engaged in to help develop student employability:

1. Embedded attribute development in the program of study, often as the result of modifications to curricula to make attribute development, job-seeking skills, and commercial awareness explicit or to accommodate employer inputs
2. Enhanced or revised central support (usually by way of the agency of career services) for undergraduates and graduates in their search for work, to which can be added provision of sectorwide resources
3. Innovative provision of work experience opportunities within, or external to, programs of study

4. Enabled reflection on and recording of experience, attribute development, and achievement alongside academic abilities, through development of "progress files" and "career management programs"

These four broad areas of development activity have in the past tended to operate in relative isolation from each other. In some areas, especially on "thin sandwich" courses (that is, programs with embedded and frequent periods of work placement or clinical practice), the integration of work experience, embedded employability development, and reflection on achievement is more marked.

However, there is now a trend toward a more holistic approach to employability development across institutions. The cultural change in higher education has seen a shift toward central support services working with program staff to help develop attributes as part of the curriculum and maximize reflection on an array of work experiences. Self-promotion and career management is no longer a separate activity but increasingly integrated into the program and linked to career planning and recording achievement. This is important as graduates must be able to do more than just sell themselves; they have to be able to perform in a job once they are recruited. Conversely, potentially good performers also need the skills to get a job in the first place. Emphasis is also being placed on learning to learn, through programs, with a shift in pedagogy from "knowing what" to "knowing how to find out," and through reflecting on work experience (Harvey, Locke, and Morey, 2002, p. x).

Embedding Employability

Increasingly there is a move to have employability explicitly identified within the mainstream curriculum—a phenomenon noted in the United States and Australia as well as the UK (Fallows and Steven, 2000). Approaches include generic skill identification at entry and development through programs (University of Bradford, 2002) and implementation of an employability framework across the institution (Sheffield Hallam University, 2004).

Although there are institution-wide developments, much embedding is still subject-focused, often driven by government funding. The Department for Education and Employment (DEE) Quality and Employability Division established discipline network projects that ran between 1996 and 1998, covering nineteen disciplines (DEE, 1998). Between 1998 and 2000 the division sponsored four "innovation and creativity in the curriculum" projects, to identify how the curriculum could be adapted to develop competencies that enable creativity (DEE, 2000). Subsequent DEE-funded key-skills projects, for example, illustrate ways in which subject areas respond to the challenge of skills and employability and addresses issues such as how to assess skills (Gravestock and Healey, 2000).

To monitor and enhance the embedding process, some institutions are undertaking employability audits to identify the extent of employability-development activity at the program and central levels. Wales pioneered this approach through a national audit under the auspices of the Higher Education Funding Council for Wales (HEFCW, 1999), which led to the request for work experience and employability plans from each institution (HEFCW, 2000). As a result, most Welsh institutions have undertaken their own follow-up audits to monitor progress and change in programs and central services.

Integration of skills in the curriculum is also being aided, in some institutions, by restructuring programs to identify outcomes or take account of subject benchmarks from the Quality Assurance Agency for Higher Education (QAA). Introduction of computerized managed learning environments offers another opportunity to embed employability in the curriculum through encouraging new pedagogical approaches to employability. Institutional researchers could take forward analysis of employability from audits of provision to evaluation of new pedagogies, and in particular the effectiveness of assessment of skill development.

Central Support

Central support for employability includes any central resource that students or staff can call on to assist in developing employability. Usually, this involves a central role for career services. Career services, in the UK, is now engaged in a much more diverse range of activities than it used to be. The traditional view is that career services offer one-on-one career advice sessions for students. In fact, in the twenty-first century it typically collates economic and job-market information, makes it available in a variety of ways, aids students in preparing for job interviews, runs workshops on a range of areas, takes responsibility for job shops for part-time, term-time, and holiday work opportunities, runs "one-stop shops" for external enquiries, participates in regional regeneration or development agencies, works in a number of ways with employers, and carries out liaison with staff (including helping prepare and run career-development modules or embedding employability in the curriculum and supporting work experience).

Recent government enquiries and research reports encourage more and better-integrated career advice and guidance activities (DEE, 2001; Universities UK/SCOP, 2002; Morey and others, 2003). If nothing else, career services, working with departments, can do a great service by helping students realize they will need to be alert to the growing and varied range of graduate opportunities.

Central support for staff attempting to integrate employability into the curriculum takes many forms, from specific help to individual lecturers wanting to enhance a module to generic resources produced centrally that can be used by lecturers and students (Leeds Metropolitan University, 2003;

UCE Careers Service, 2002). In several institutions, central career services, lifelong learning departments, and academic staff collaborate to develop employability skills in programs and where appropriate share delivery (Oakey, Doyle, and Smith, 2000). Institutional researchers also have another role in examining the extent of involvement of central services and assessing the effectiveness of collaboration between central departments and the interrelationship between central services and academic schools.

Work Experience

Employers tend to be favorably disposed to work experience as something that helps students prepare for rapid effectiveness (Harvey, Moon, and Geall, 1997; Rover Group, 1998; Purcell, Pitcher, and Simm, 1999; Sewell, 2001; Lambert and others, 2001). Work experience provides a foretaste of workplace culture as well as contributing to learning. There is a growing trend to recruiting from students who have undertaken work placement with companies.

Employers' positive view of work experience is supported by statistical analysis of first-destination employment returns, furnished by the Higher Education Statistics Agency, for all full-time degree qualifiers from all higher education institutions in the United Kingdom in 1995–96 (Bowes and Harvey, 2000). The results of the study are based on aggregated figures. The first-destination returns are collected only six months after graduation and so the employment rate may not reflect the longer-term pattern in a subject area. An operational sample of thirty-three subject areas involving 74,922 graduates was used to examine the impact of work experience. Overall, graduates from sandwich courses (that is, those programs where a student has an embedded year out in a work setting) had a higher postgraduation employment rate (69.1 percent) than students on equivalent nonsandwich courses (55.3 percent). This advantage is dependent on subject area: science and language sandwich graduates, for instance, did not enjoy a significant advantage but most built-environment, business, engineering, and social science sandwich graduates did.

A study of nearly two thousand art and design graduates from fourteen British institutions in the mid-1990s (Harvey and Blackwell, 1999) revealed that respondents who had undertaken a work-experience placement had a higher rate of full-time permanent employment after graduation. They also had a more favorable view of the undergraduate program and belief that their employability skills had been more strongly developed in the undergraduate years. Those with work experience that was related to their current job also tended to earn a higher income. These results are mirrored in the "Working Out?" study: "Nearly 48 percent of graduates felt that relevant work experience in a similar organization was an important factor in enabling them to obtain their job" (Purcell, Pitcher, and Simm, 1999, p. 16).

The Dearing report placed considerable emphasis on work experience, concluding among other things that "students can benefit from experience in many different settings, structured and informal, paid and unpaid" (NCIHE, 1997). Employers also benefit from work experience by having staff develop as mentors and enablers, as well as building up links with higher education institutions (Blackwell and others, 2000). The National Council for Work Experience was established to promote work experience and established a dedicated support Web site (NCWE, 2005).

Work experience can take a variety of forms, among them traditional placements through "live" project work and part-time employment. Three main categories of work experience can be identified (Harvey and others, 1998; CSU/NCWE, 1999; Little and others, 2001):

1. Organized work experience as part of a program of study
2. Organized work experience external to a program of study
3. Ad hoc work experience external to a program of study

There is some overlap among the categories. Voluntary work, for example, can sometimes be accredited by an institution, is sometimes organized externally to the program of study, or may be ad hoc work undertaken by students.

Work Experience as Part of the Program. There are three main variants of work experience as part of a program of study. The first is a conventional program with some work-experience element attached to it, as an optional or compulsory component. This includes traditional one-year placement on a sandwich course, a short period of work experience on a nonsandwich program, clinical or practice placement on some professional degrees, live project working, and collaboration between students and employers (which does not involve a placement but visits to and close working with employers). In addition, work shadowing linked to programs of study also afford exposure of a limited type.

Second, there are generic work-experience modules available to students in a range of programs. These include year-long placement unconnected to a specific program; credit for part-time, term-time, or vacation work; credit for voluntary (unpaid) work; as well as programs developed by student unions for elected officers. Generic modules are often assessed and count toward the final award. They may also attract separate accreditation (University of Wales, Aberystwyth, 2002; University College Chester, 2002; Highton, 2003).

Third, work experience may be through a program that is wholly, or predominantly, delivered in the workplace setting. This includes professional learning in the form of continuing professional development, accreditation of prior experiential learning, and graduate apprenticeship (DEE, 1998, 1999; Bowers-Brown and others, 2003).

Organized Work Experience External to the Program. Students also undertake organized work experience external to the program of study. The range of such opportunities includes programs such as the Careers Research and Advisory Centre's Insight Plus (2002), Shell Technology Enterprise Programme (STEP; 2005), and Business Bridge (2002).

Another form of external organized work experience is voluntary work through Community Service Volunteers (2003), Millennium Volunteers, or Student Volunteering UK (2005). There are about twenty-five thousand student volunteers across the UK working in community-based projects in more than 180 further education and higher education volunteering groups (Speakman, Drake, and Hawkins, 2001). Most top employers prefer to recruit candidates who have undertaken voluntary work experience (Reed Executive, 2001).

Ad Hoc Work Experience. Students obtain work experience through casual, part-time, or vacation work, or for part-time students through their own full-time employment or other activities. Institutionally based surveys found that the majority of students already had work experience before entering higher education (Work Experience Bank, 1998). Surveys show that 50–60 percent of full-time students work during term time and probably 80 percent of full-time students work over the summer vacation. The indications are that the proportion of full-time students working is increasing and that they are working on average around ten to fourteen hours a week during term time (Daniel, 2002; Barclays Bank, 2001; Callender and Kemp, 2000; Newell and Winn, 2000; Unite/Mori, 2000; Smith and Taylor, 1999; National Union of Students, 1999; Walker, 1999; Taylor, 1998; Rover Group, 1998; Lucas and Ralston, 1997; Hallowell, 1995; Paton-Saltzberg and Lindsay, 1995; Mason and Harvey, 1995; Ford, Bosworth, and Wilson, 1995; Edmundson and Carpenter, 1994). The increase in part-time working is greatest among low-income and older students, those living at home with their parents, female students (especially from ethnic minorities), and those attending a university in London or Scotland or attending university after 1992. Students from low-income families also tend to work longer hours (Callender, 2001a, 2001b; Connor and others, 2001; Metcalf, 2001; Barke and others, 2000; Callender and Kemp, 2000).

Traditionally, part-time working during term time was seen as interfering with academic work ("Part-Time Working . . . ," 1998; Brennan and Shah, 2002). Now, most universities run job clubs for students or support the student search for part-time work. In some places, as noted earlier, the learning from part-time work is being taken more seriously and given credit. This changing view toward part-time working is indicative of pragmatic acceptance of students' need to work while studying because state support is no longer sufficient. Rather than ignore it or regard it negatively, academics are trying to get students to think positively about what they learn from their part-time work. This, to some extent, differs from the U.S.

situation, where part-time working has always been a facet of the student experience and continues to be seen somewhat negatively as increasing time to graduation. Institutional researchers might undertake studies of students' paid or voluntary work to monitor the level of work and change over time. This could be set alongside opportunities for work experience embedded in programs and take-up of external organized work experience.

Learning from Work Experience

The *Work Experience* report (Harvey, Geall, and Moon, 1998) argued that experience of work should not be regarded as something intrinsically beneficial. On the contrary, it is the learning that comes from the experience that is important. This view now appears to predominate within higher education institutions and is reflected, for example, in the approach adopted by the National Council for Work Experience (NCWE, 2002), InsightPlus (CRAC, 2002), and the National Union of Students (1999).

Learning from work experience is effective if:

- It is meaningful or relevant to future career development
- It is planned and intentional from the outset
- It is assessed or accredited and integrated into undergraduate programs
- The quality is monitored and employers, participating academics, and students are all committed to it
- It adds to a work-experience portfolio, as with a mixture of course-embedded placements and part-time working
- There is a process for articulation and reflection

In most instances, where students have formal work experience placement, there is an established procedure for monitoring and aiding reflection, especially if the placement is accredited or successful completion is necessary for progression (QAA, 2001a).

Reflection and Recording Achievement

The most recent developments in the new, integrated approach to employability have been in structuring and encouraging reflection, in particular through processes enabling students to record achievement as part of personal development planning. Part of the developmental framework for higher education is introduction of progress files, which include a transcript of formal learning and achievement, an individual's reflection and recording of personal development, and career planning. Progress files "support the concept that learning is a lifetime activity" (QAA, 2002).

Personal development planning (PDP) is an important element of the progress file and should be operational across the whole higher education system in the UK by 2005–06 (QAA, 2001b). The intention of PDP is to help students (QAA, 2002):

- Become more effective, independent, and confident self-directed learners
- Understand how they are learning and relate their learning to a wider context
- Improve their general skills for study and career management
- Articulate personal goals and evaluate progress toward achievement
- Encourage a positive attitude to learning throughout life

There are various ways of implementing PDP, notably using the personal tutor system, embedding reflection on skills development in the curriculum, and linking reflection to assessment (Drew and Bingham, 2001; Cottrell, 2003). Student diversity requires flexibility in approach; what is suitable to a recent school leaver may not be appropriate for a mature student (Ward and Pierce, 2003), and the requirements of international students may differ from those of domestic students. Institutional researchers might, in the first instance, monitor the extent and nature of implementation of PDP, and subsequently evaluate student engagement and the value students' place on the PDP process.

Career Management

A significant change in higher education in the UK has been a focus on students' own career management skills. The Career Management Skills Programme created by the Careers Research and Advisory Centre was a pioneer in encouraging students to begin planning and managing their future career early on, while at university. CRAC (2002) developed InsightPlus as a national scheme that sought to increase student employability by aiding students' recognition of the skills they develop while undertaking part-time employment or voluntary work.

Conclusions

The requirements of employers are sometimes seen to be at odds with those of academia. Closer analysis of what employers are looking for reveals congruity between the abilities developed in higher education and those desired by employers (Harvey and Knight, 1996).

The last five years have witnessed an accelerating pace of engagement with employability within the academy. Initial, piecemeal accommodation of employability through skills modules has developed into a more diverse array of opportunities. In some institutions, they have developed into an integrated, holistic strategy, most recently linked to learning and teaching policy.

However, developments are not uniform across the sector. One well-placed commentator, a curriculum developer in a prestigious bricks-and-mortar university, recently noted: "I think you will find fairly universally that in terms of embedding employability and work-based learning in the curriculum, the red brick universities have some serious catching up to do with their new university/ex-poly counterparts."

The variations across the sector reflect experience in developing employability rather than segmentation of mission. Embedding and integrating employability development initiatives has moved to center stage for all institutions. Nonetheless, many activities in institutions are primed through various nationally funded initiatives. This is a problem for developing and maintaining an integrated strategy. Although externally funded initiatives can be extremely useful in kick-starting activity, they could have only limited impact if perceived as transitory or marginal. Such initiatives often lead to activity for a couple of years before the process dies from lack of funding. In some cases, an initiative is extended by being embedded in institutional processes and culture. However, it is often difficult to track down what has become of a funded initiative. External money from government schemes is welcome provided it does not lead to short-term, inconsequential, initiative chasing. One positive development that has been taken up in both pre- and post-1992 universities is the development of Centres for Excellence in Teaching and Learning (CETL) in employability, which commence operation in 2005 and are funded for five years in the first instance.

It is important that, in the last resort, employability development be driven bottom-up by staff and students and that institutional management provide the context to allow such initiatives to thrive. Monitoring and aiding this process is an important task for institutional researchers.

References

Barclays Bank. *Barclays Student Survey 2001*. London: Barclays Bank, 2001.

Barke, M., Braidford, P., Houston, M., Hunt, A., Lincoln, I., Morphet, C., Stone, I., and Walker, A. *Students in the Labour Market: Nature, Extent and Implications of Term-Time Employment Among University of Northumbria Undergraduates*. Research report RR 215. London: Department for Education and Employment (DEE), 2000.

Blackwell, A., Bowes, L., Harvey, L., Hesketh, A. J., and Knight, P. T. "Transforming Work Experience in Higher Education." *British Educational Research Journal*, 2000, 27(3), 269–286.

Blasko, Z., Brennan, J., Little, B., and Shah, T. *Access to What?: Analysis of Factors Determining Graduate Employability*. Bristol: Higher Education Funding Council for England, 2002.

Bowers-Brown, T., Norman, L., Harvey, L., Knight, P., Little, B., and Yorke, M. "A Review of the Graduate Apprenticeship Scheme." Report to Higher Education Funding Council for England by Enhancing Student Employability Co-Ordination Team (ESECT), Bristol, 2003.

Bowes, L., and Harvey, L. *The Impact of Sandwich Education on the Activities of Graduates Six Months Post-Graduation*. London: National Centre for Work Experience and Center for Research into Quality, 2000.

Brennan, J., and Shah, T., *Access to What? How to Convert Educational Opportunity into Employment Opportunity for Groups from Disadvantaged Backgrounds. Interim Report on Phase 2*. London: Centre for Higher Education Research and Information, 2002.

Burrows, A., Harvey, L., and Green, D. *Is Anybody Listening? Employers' Views on Quality in Higher Education (2nd ed.).* Birmingham, England: QHE, 1992.

Business Bridge. Web site. Retrieved July 28, 2005, http://www.business-bridge.org.uk. 2002.

Callender, C. *The Impact of Student Debt on Participation and Term-Time Employment on Attainment: What Can Research Tell Us? A Summary.* London: Universities UK, CHERI, and South Bank University, 2001a.

Callender, C. "Supplementary Memorandum Appendix 36 Higher Education: Student Retention." Retrieved July 28, 2005, http://www.parliament.the-stationery-office.co. uk/pa/cm200001/cmselect/cmeduemp/124/124ap44.htm. 2001b.

Callender, C., and Kemp, M. *Changing Student Finances: Income, Expenditure and Take-up of Student Loans Among Full- and Part-time Higher Education Students in 1998–89.* London: DEE, 2000.

Cannon, T. "View from Industry." In G. C. Moodie (ed.), *Standards and Criteria in Higher Education.* Guildford, England: Society for Research into Higher Education (SRHE) and NFER/Nelson, 1986.

Careers Research and Advisory Centre (CRAC). "InsightPlus." Retrieved July 28, 2005, http://www.insightplus.co.uk. 2002.

Careers Service Unit and National Council for Work Experience (CSU/NCWE). "What Is Work?" In *Focus on Work Experience.* Manchester, England: CSU, 1999.

Collective Enterprise Ltd. (CEL). "The Experience of Recent Graduates in IT, Electronics and Communications (ICET)." Summary paper, Conference Centre, Victoria Street, London, Apr. 18, 2002.

Community Service Volunteers. Web site. Visited July 28, 2005, http://www.csv.org.uk/. 2003.

Connor, H., Dawson, S., Tyers, C., Eccles, J., Regan, J., and Aston, J. *Social Class and Higher Education: Issues Affecting Decisions on Participation by Lower Social Class Groups.* Research report RR 267. London: DEE, 2001.

Cottrell, S. *Skills for Success: The Personal Development Planning Handbook.* London: Palgrave Macmillan, 2003.

Council for Industry and Higher Education (CIHE). *Rates of Return to Qualifications: A Summary of Recent Evidence.* London: CIHE, 2002.

Daniel, A. "Working for Yourself? Employability Study among Fine Art and Jewellery and Silversmithing Students 2001–02." Birmingham, Birmingham Institute of Art and Design, University of Central England in Birmingham, 2002.

de la Harpe, B., Radloff, A., and Wyber, J. "Quality and Generic (Professional) Skills." *Quality in Higher Education,* 2000, 6(3) 231–243.

Department for Education and Employment (DEE). "Quality and Employability Division, 1996–98, Discipline Network Projects." Retrieved July 28, 2005, http://www.dfes.gov.uk/dfee/heqe/discnetprojs.htm. 1998.

Department for Education and Employment (DEE). *Higher Education: Quality and Employability Digest.* Sheffield, England: DEE, 1999.

Department for Education and Employment (DEE). "Higher Education Digest Special Issue on Higher Education Development Projects." Retrieved July 28, 2005, http://www.dfes.gov.uk/dfee/heqe/cheri_dfee_digest.pdf. 2000.

Department for Education and Employment (DEE). *Developing Modern Higher Education Careers Services.* Nottingham, England: DEE Publications, 2001.

Drew, S., and Bingham, R. *The Student Skills Guide.* Aldershot, England: Gower, 2001.

Edmundson, T., and Carpenter, C. *University of Westminster Students' Financial Circumstances Report 1994.* London: University of Westminster, 1994.

Egerton, M. "Mature Graduates I: Occupational Attainment and the Effects of Labour Market Duration." *Oxford Review of Education,* 2001, 27(1), 135–150.

Fallows, S., and Steven, C. *Integrating Key Skills in Higher Education: Employability, Transferable Skills and Learning for Life.* London: Kogan Page, 2000.

Ford, J., Bosworth, D., and Wilson, R. "Part-Time Work and Full-Time Higher Education." *Studies in Higher Education,* 1995, *20*(2), 187–202.

Gravestock, P., and Healey, M. *Key Skills in Geography in Higher Education.* Cheltenham, England: Geography and Environmental Management Research Unit, Cheltenham and Gloucester College of Higher Education, 2000.

Hallowell, S. *Student Finance Survey 1994/5.* Leicester, England: Leicester University, 1995.

Harvey, L., "Defining and Measuring Employability." *Quality in Higher Education,* 2001, *7*(2), 97–109.

Harvey, L., and Blackwell, A. "Gender Bias in Incomes of Art and Design Graduates." *Industry and Higher Education,* 1999, *13*(5), 323–329.

Harvey, L., Geall, V., and Moon, S., with Aston, J., Bowes, L., and Blackwell, A. *Work Experience: Expanding Opportunities for Undergraduates.* Birmingham, England: Centre for Research into Quality, 1998.

Harvey, L., and Knight, P. T. *Transforming Higher Education.* Buckingham, England: Society for Research into Higher Education (SRHE) and Open University Press, 1996.

Harvey, L., Locke, W., and Morey, A. "Enhancing Employability, Recognising Diversity: Making Links Between Higher Education and the World of Work." Retrieved July 28, 2005, http://www.universitiesuk.ac.uk/bookshop/downloads/employability.pdf. 2002.

Harvey, L., Moon, S., and Geall, V., with Bower, R. *Graduates' Work: Organization Change and Students' Attributes.* Birmingham, England: Centre for Research into Quality and Association of Graduate Recruiters (AGR), 1997.

Higher Education Funding Council for Wales (HEFCW). "Pilot Audit of Employability Provision in Higher Education Institutions in Wales." Cardiff: HEFCW, 1999.

Higher Education Funding Council for Wales (HEFCW). "Work Experience and Employability Plans." Retrieved July 28, 2005, http://www.wfc.ac.uk/education/hefcw/pub00/w0052he.html. 2000.

Highton, M. *Reflection in Work-Based Learning for Undergraduates.* Edinburgh, Scotland: Napier University, 2003.

Johnson, D., Pere-Vergé, L., and Hanage, R. "Graduate Retention and the Regional Economy." *Entrepreneurship and Regional Development,* 1993, *5,* 85–97.

Lambert, E., Scarles, C., Marlow-Hayne, N., Blakeman, A., Morey, A., and Harvey, L. "Employability and the Media Studies Curriculum, Report to a Consortium of Four Universities." Birmingham: CRQ, 2001.

Learning and Teaching Support Network (LTSN) Generic Centre. "Learning and Employability Series of Papers." Retrieved July 28, 2005, http://www.heacademy.ac.uk/1433.htm. 2003.

Leeds Metropolitan University. "Skills for Learning." Retrieved July 28, 2005, http://www.leedsmet.ac.uk/lskills/. 2003.

Lees, D. "Graduate Employability: Literature Review." Retrieved July 28, 2005, http://www.heacademy.ac.uk/resources.asp?process=full_record&section=generic&id=190. 2002.

Little, B., Moon, S., Pierce, D., Harvey, L., and Marlow-Hayne, N. *Nature and Extent of Undergraduates' Work Experience.* London: CIHE/DFES, 2001.

Lucas, R., and Ralston, L. "Youth, Gender and Part-Time Employment. A Preliminary Appraisal of Student Employment." *Employee Relations,* 1997, *19*(1), 51–66.

Mansergh, T. P. "The Relationship of Occupational Skills and Attributes in Work Situations to Salary and Occupation." Unpublished M.Ed. thesis, University of New England, Armidale, NSW, Australia, 1990.

Mason, S., and Harvey, L. "Funding Higher Education: Student Perspectives." Birmingham: Centre for Research into Quality, University of Central England in Birmingham, 1995.

Medhat, S. "A New Beginning for a Strained Relationship." *Times Higher Education Supplement,* Jan. 24, 2003, p. 18.

Metcalf, H. "Increasing Inequality in Higher Education: The Role of Term-Time Working." Unpublished report. London: National Institute of Economic and Social Research, 2001.

Morey, A., Harvey, L., Williams, J., Saldana, A., and Mena, P. *HE Careers Services and Diversity: How Careers Advisory Services Can Enhance the Employability of Graduates from Non-Traditional Backgrounds.* Manchester, England: HECSU, 2003.

National Committee of Inquiry into Higher Education (NCIHE). *Higher Education in the Learning Society.* London: Her Majesty's Stationery Office (HMSO), 1997.

National Council for Work Experience (NCWE). *Work Related Learning Report.* Nottingham: DES, 2002.

National Council for Work Experience (NCWE). "Welcome to work-experience.org." Retrieved July 28, 2005, http://www.work-experience.org. 2005.

National Union of Students. *Student Hardship Survey.* London: NUS, 1999.

Newell, C., and Winn, S. *The Financial Situation of Students at the University of Brighton: The Ninth Report, 1999/2000.* Brighton, England: Health and Social Policy Research Centre, University of Brighton, 2000.

Oakey, D., Doyle, M., and Smith, J. "A Strategic Approach to Undergraduate Key Skills Development: Salford Key Skills Project, Final Report." Salford, England: University of Salford, 2000.

"Part-Time Working Can Harm Studies." *Times Higher Education Supplement* (THES), Jan. 23, 1998.

Paton-Saltzberg, R., and Lindsay, R. O. *The Effects of Paid Employment on the Academic Performance of Full-Time Students in Higher Education. A Report of a Study Commissioned by the Academic Standards Committee of Oxford Brookes University.* Oxford, England: Oxford Brookes University, 1995.

Purcell, K., Pitcher, J., and Simm, C. *Working Out? Graduates' Early Experience of the Labour Market.* Manchester, England: Careers Service Unit, 1999.

Quality Assurance Agency for Higher Education (QAA). "Code of Practice on Placement Learning." Retrieved July 28, 2005, http://www.qaa.ac.uk/academicinfrastructure/code OfPractice/section9/default.asp. 2001a.

Quality Assurance Agency for Higher Education (QAA). "Guidelines for HE Progress Files." Retrieved July 28, 2005, http://www.qaa.ac.uk/academicinfrastructure/ progressFiles/guidelines/progfile2001.asp. 2001b.

Quality Assurance Agency for Higher Education (QAA). "Progress Files for Higher Education." Retrieved July 28, 2005, http://www.qaa.ac.uk/crntwork/progfilehe/contents.htm. 2002.

Reed Executive. *British Firms Rate Voluntary Work.* London: Band and Brown, 2001.

Rover Group. "Young People Development Survey, 1997." Rover Group, 1998.

Sewell, P. "Higher Level Skills in Creative Industries in Lancashire and Cumbria." Retrieved July 28, 2005, http://www.lmi4he.ac.uk/Documents/Brief26.doc. 2001.

Sheffield Hallam University. "Employability Framework." Policy document. Sheffield, England: Sheffield Hallam University, 2004.

Shell Technology Enterprise Program (STEP). STEP Web site. Visited July 28, 2005, http://www.step.org.uk/. 2005.

Smith, N., and Taylor, P. "Not for Lipstick and Lager: Students and Part-Time Work." *Scottish Affairs Journal,* 1999, *28,* 147–163.

Speakman, Z., Drake, K., and Hawkins, P. *The Art of Crazy Paving, Student Volunteering.* London: DES Publications, 2001.

Student Volunteering UK. Web site. Visited July 28, 2005, http://www.studentvol. org.uk/. 2005.

Taylor, N. K. "Survey of Paid Employment Undertaken by Full-Time Undergraduates at an Established Scottish University." *Journal of Further and Higher Education,* 1998, 22(1), 33–40.

Unite/Mori. *Student Living Report.* Bristol, England: Unite, 2000.

Universities UK/SCOP. *Student Services: Effective Approaches to Retaining Students in Higher Education.* London: Universities UK, 2002.

University of Bradford. "Excellence Plus: Developing Key Skills for the Future." Retrieved July 28, 2005, http://www.bradford.ac.uk/excellenceplus/future.php. 2002.

University of Central England in Birmingham (UCE) Careers Service. "Delivering Employability: A Framework for Career Development in the Curriculum." Retrieved July 28, 2005, http://www.ssv.uce.ac.uk/Careers/car-staff-employ-deliver.htm. 2002.

University College Chester. *New Centre Designed to Meet the Needs of Businesses in Cheshire.* Chester, England: University College Chester, 2002.

University of Wales, Aberystwyth. "Year in Employment Scheme." Retrieved July 28, 2005, http://www.aber.ac.uk/careers/yes/. 2002.

Walker, L. "Longitudinal Study of Drop-Out and Continuing Students Who Attended the Pre-University Summer School at the University of Glasgow." *International Journal of Lifelong Education,* 1999, *18*(3), 217–233.

Ward, R., and Pierce, D. "Employability and Students' Educational Experiences Before Entering Higher Education." Retrieved July 28, 2005, http://www.heacademy.ac.uk/resources.asp?process=full_record&section=generic&id=234. 2003.

Work Experience Bank. *Students' Work: A Study of the Work Experience of Students.* Sheffield, England: DEE, 1998.

LEE HARVEY is professor and director of the Centre for Research and Evaluation at Sheffield Hallam University, United Kingdom.

3

This chapter offers techniques that can help institutional researchers play a more active role in the process of creating and modifying instructional programs to meet workforce needs.

Institutional Research and New Program Development

Richard A. Voorhees

At most institutions, more energy is expended on maintaining an inventory of existing programs than on adjusting them or even creating new ones to better meet market needs. Where an external review process exists, fear of program discontinuation has generated great concern and spurred time-consuming effort to collect a variety of *internal* data on trends in student credit hours, faculty productivity, graduation rate, and outcome data on graduate placement. All this activity subtracts from the energy necessary to gather *external* data that can be used to alter an existing program or test the viability of a new one.

Institutional researchers have traditionally played a fundamental role in gathering internal data for use in program review. In this chapter, I argue that institutional research offices can assume a larger role in institutional health by gathering and analyzing data, chiefly external, to guide institutions through the process of program generation. Although program review presents a structure for scaling down and eliminating programs, careful assessment of market opportunities holds the promise of strengthening institutional vitality. This chapter offers a framework for assessing the market potential for new programs relying on techniques that should be in the arsenal of most professional institutional researchers.

Note: Portions of this chapter previously appeared in Voorhees, R., "Assessing the Market Potential for New Academic Programs." In R. S. Lay and J. J. Endo (eds.), *Designing and Using Market Research*. New Directions for Institutional Research, no. 54. San Francisco: Jossey-Bass, 1988.

Program-Market Opportunity Matrix

Kotler and Fox (1995) recommend that institutions identify market potential through use of a program-market opportunity matrix. This nine-cell matrix allows an institution to place present and future programs along two dimensions: markets (existing, geographical, new) and programs (existing, modified, and new). This matrix yields terms associated with market potential that are used in this chapter:

- *Existing program development.* This consists of deeper penetration of existing markets, geographical expansion, or finding new market segments for existing programs. This is what many institutions do under the rubric of "marketing"; that is, colleges increase their promotion of existing programs or search for new market segments for existing programs.
- *Program modification.* This occurs when an institution modifies programs with either existing or new markets in mind. The natural tendency of most institutions when faced with an enrollment shortfall is to repackage existing courses and programs under other labels and offer them at differing times and in varying formats in order to attract students. This process can promote short-term institutional survival but may not produce the fundamental change in programs necessary for long-term institutional health.
- *New program development.* This refers to the process of creating new programs for existing, modified, or totally new markets. Total innovation occurs when an institution decides to create new classes, departments, or schools designed specifically for new markets. Creation of "universities without walls" during the 1960s and 1970s represents total innovation because of the focus on serving hitherto underserved populations of nontraditional students.

Points of Departure

Institutions embarking on a path leading to program modification or new program development must ask a series of interrelated yet fundamental questions at the outset. First, what is the relationship between current programs and a proposed new one? New programs must be balanced with existing offerings to ensure that the new mix is compatible with existing structures. A new degree program usually requires a general education component that must be accommodated through "service" courses. A certificate, or short-term training program, may carry no requirement for general education. A new program, particularly one planned for market segments with special needs (for instance, low-income single mothers), may also require new college services. Given a documented need, will college trustees, the administration, and the faculty be willing to add to or modify service classes and student services to accommodate new market segments?

Second, what type of student will be served by the proposed program? A new program may attract a new type, resulting in a change in the composition of the student body. The opposite is true as well; a new program may appeal only to a narrow cross-section of current students and fail to attract new ones. Introduction of a dissimilar program may be perceived as an affront by current students, faculty, alumni, and other important publics. The development of the program may not hinge on the perception of current students, faculty, staff, and other stakeholders, but certainly changes in the campus and organizational culture should be among the factors accounted for in new program development.

Third, what is the impact of the proposed program on institutional resources? Even if totally self-supporting in the short run, campus constituencies may view a new program as diverting resources from existing ones. If a commitment has been made to preserve the status quo, overwhelming evidence to the contrary, an institution may be unable to afford new programs even in the best of circumstances.

Finally, how does the proposed program fit with the institutional role and mission? Operating in a financially constrained environment, most governing boards will hardly grant approval to new initiatives they do not perceive to be consonant with the institutional role and mission. The search for answers to these questions is the starting point in any process of new program development. The techniques described here can bring other questions into clearer focus.

Techniques to Assess the Market Potential of New Programs

Techniques used to develop instructional programs should be structured to answer two central questions: Is there a pool of prospective students who are likely to enroll? What is the market for program graduates? In the United States, fortunately, a variety of publications and datasets readily available through the Internet can begin to address both answers.

First, in addition to the major census conducted every ten years the U.S. Census Bureau updates demographic information periodically by location. For institutions that draw students from regional or national markets, state summaries of census data may be aggregated. For those serving an explicitly defined geographical area, census data are reported by more discrete units termed *census tracts*, the boundaries of which are configured so that they contain an average of four thousand people.

Second, government and quasi-governmental agencies—regional governmental planning agencies, state labor departments, legislative clearing houses—use census data and data developed by the research arms of private and nonprofit entities to prepare reports on demographic and employment trends. Given a sufficient rationale, these agencies can also prepare reports customized to institutional specifications.

Third, chambers of commerce, banks, utility companies, and similar agencies and employers operating within a given geographical area generate reports that focus on demographic trends, employment data, and economic forecasts. These information sources can give institutions the basic data needed to begin addressing the question of where new students can be found; the sources can serve as an indicator of employment opportunities for students enrolled in programs leading directly to careers. As a starting point, this off-the-shelf data can illuminate other potential questions necessary for program development. Institutional research offices can help their institutions through maintaining digital collections of these data for rapid extraction as requested by administrators and other stakeholders who are interested in external trends.

Surveys of Prospective Students. Most institutions conduct surveys of potential employers; few survey prospective students. Lack of information about prospective students is a significant shortcoming in assessing the market potential for a new program. At a minimum, a survey of prospective students seeks to identify the demographic characteristics, educational aspirations, and current education level of respondents. At the most, the study also seeks to determine preferences for any specific type of instruction, scheduling choice, the extent to which information on existing programming reaches its intended audience, and perception of institutional image. In addition to profiling career-related preferences, surveys of this nature can also point to the desire to increase general knowledge in liberal arts areas. A random survey of adults residing in Arapahoe Community College's service area in Colorado (Voorhees and Hart, 1985) was instrumental in pointing to market potential. The Arapahoe study found, among other adult educational preferences, that as the respondent's age increased so did the perceived need for classes in the liberal arts. Also crucial to the college's planning for off-campus classes and services was the finding that 77 percent of all adults surveyed indicated they would not drive more than ten miles to attend college classes. Although specific results may have changed in the last twenty years, such surveys still serve a major role in identifying trends, needs, and preferences and can help an institution better plan its offerings.

Surveys of Current Students. The opinions and aspirations of currently enrolled students and the insights they might offer about program development are often overlooked in the new program development process. Since these students are currently enrolled in one or more college classes, they are easily accessible and serve as a microcosm of the opinions of new students. It is reasonable to expect that the perceptions current students hold about such institutional services as job placement, parking, and child care do not differ significantly from those of new students. Perceptions of institutional image and the quality of campus life may, however, differ with the socioeconomic background, previous educational experience, and age of prospective students.

Several commercially available instruments can supplement an institution's efforts to capture student attitudes and opinions through a home-grown instrument. They include the American College Testing Service's Evaluation Survey Service (ESS), the Cooperative Institutional Research Program (CIRP) surveys developed by the Higher Education Research Institute at the University of California at Los Angeles, and the Student-Outcomes Information Service (SOIS) surveys developed by the National Center for Higher Education Management Systems and the College Entrance Examination Board. In the UK, the well-established Student Satisfaction Approach initially developed at the University of Central England is an adaptable and portable technique that can serve such purposes.

Several newer instruments, notably the National Survey of Student Engagement (NSSE) and its counterpart the Community College Survey of Student Engagement (CCSSE), assess among other factors student perception of institutional practices that are highly correlated with student learning and retention. Institutional researchers can glean important clues from these normative instruments that inform the total institution, and where their authors have made it possible to identify a respondent by returning a student identifier to the institution, important information is fed back to existing programs. At most campuses, the institutional research office is deeply involved in surveying students and can serve as the place where trends are monitored.

Market Segmentation. The past two decades have been marked by rapid improvement in market research spawned by technology. Until the 1970s, market research in the private sector was dominated by demographic segmentation—that is, classification of potential consumers by age, income, level of education, and other quantitative variables. The emergence of the baby boomers (whose consumer habits were radically different from those of previous generations) and the disappearance of the captive housewife (as more women entered the workforce) contributed to the demise of demographic research as the sole technique for determining target markets; people were no longer behaving or consuming products in ways that traditional research could explain. Moving from demographic segmentation through geographic segmentation and now to psychographic segmentation, market research has assumed a mantle of sophistication brought about by increased access to data and accelerated use of survey research.

Values and Lifestyles Typology (VALS). The Values and Lifestyles Typology (Scientific Research International, 2003) is an example of lifestyle research that has evolved since it first appeared in the late 1970s. Primarily used to predict consumer behavior, VALS can serve academic planners as an additional tool to gauge corresponding interest in a given program's proposed content or format. VALS divides adults into eight consumer types, identified by lifestyle. These types, or segments, are grouped into four lifestyle categories on the basis of attitudes, consumption patterns, demographics, and resources available for consumer expenditures.

VALS research, for instance, suggests that "achievers," with their goal-oriented lifestyle, focus first on family and career, avoiding situations that produce a high degree of stimulation and change. Achievers also prefer premium products that demonstrate success. Knowing this, academic planners may wish to match programs to this segment that are short-term, available conveniently (perhaps online courses), and carry prestige. "Experiencers" are searching for the unconventional and might be best matched with programs that differ from traditional academic fare, perhaps a hybrid program that emphasizes new societal trends. "Survivors," because of their lack of higher education and despairing attitudes, would be the most difficult group to match with new programs. Alternatively, "innovators" have usually completed a college education but come back to the college classroom to further their interest in leadership, especially as it applies to new techniques and technologies. Scheduling options, delivery mechanisms, and even program content designed for these groups would need to be significantly different.

Psychographic Research. Psychographics represents a refinement of lifestyle research. By structuring more operational dimensions underlying consumer behavior than lifestyle research does, more precision is brought to marketing efforts. Psychographics estimates consumer interests, activities, and values and plots these dimensions with reference to demographics. One simply needs to search the Internet for *psychographic research* to know that this area has become a big business. The underlying demographic and geographic data for these services is taken from periodic surveys undertaken by the U.S. Census Bureau as well as proprietary databases sampling consumer behavior.

In addition to information that an institution can find for free from the U.S. Census Bureau for a given jurisdiction (median income, household size, average home value, age, education status, employment by sector, and gender), commercial psychographic firms can also furnish estimates of the amount spent on a variety of goods and services by households residing in the area of interest. These data then can be segmented by lifestyle descriptors that allow decision makers a fuller picture of potential learners residing in a given area. Environmental Systems Research Institute (ESRI, 2004), for example, can combine consumer choice data according to two or more of sixty-six "community tapestry" segments. Of these segments, several are identified with readily seeking more education.

Psychographics research can be costly. It may also not differentiate among consumers at the lowest level of analysis (in other words, at the block level). Even with these limitations, however, psychographics can offer insight into potential learning markets that has been heretofore unavailable to institutions that rely solely on demographic profiles. Psychographics also makes heavy use of geographic information systems (GIS) mapping, allowing a visual overlay of consumer characteristics and attitudes to produce a spatial representation of target markets.

Employment Surveys and Studies. The employer survey, in which employers are asked to estimate their future need for trained personnel, is the most popular type of study for determining the marketability of career program graduates (Table 3.1). Employer surveys are used most often in local markets because the proximity of employers to the institution ensures a higher rate of return. Properly conducted, these surveys can be the first step in involving employers in program development. Employer estimates of personnel requirements, however, often suffer from reliability and validity problems. This is especially true among smaller employers who might lack the expertise to anticipate future technological developments that affect their position within a given employment field.

Less frequent among employment surveys are econometric studies, in which an array of input variables are used to model demand by occupational category over a ten-year period. These studies, produced by the Bureau of Labor Statistics, U.S. Department of Labor, are perhaps more reliable and valid than institutionally produced employer studies. However, they are built on assumptions that forecast productivity, consumption, and overall economic output, each of which may be expected to vary widely or at least unpredictably over the course of ten years. As recent decades have abundantly proven, forecasting technological change or economic trends is at best a risky business. For this reason, many organizations have turned to environmental scanning as a strategic planning technique. Environmental scanning can give decision makers information on the latest developments in key issues related to organizational survival, including unfolding trends in technology, employment rate, relocation of major industries, productivity rate, and consumer patterns. One can easily see how environmental scanning can inform all phases of program development in general, and econometric studies, trend extrapolation research, and job vacancy studies in particular.

Program Need Index. For schools operating in geographical areas where more than one institution produces graduates in a given field, the Program Need Index (PNI) suggested by Nielsen (1981) may be a useful technique for assessing the feasibility of initiating a new program. Used cautiously, the PNI allows an institution to compare the relative strength of current and proposed programs in a geographically defined labor market while accounting for the presence or absence of similar programs offered at competing institutions. The PNI is given by a formula:

$$PNI = \frac{\text{Number of current employees in targeted employment area}}{\text{Number of graduates in area with related majors}}$$

For program planning purposes, the value computed for the PNI should exceed 1. Values lower than 1 indicate that there are more programs producing graduates in a given geographical area than the labor market can

Table 3.1. Employment Surveys and Study Techniques for Program Development

Type	Purpose	Advantages	Disadvantages
Industry survey	Determines all possible jobs within a given industry; points to all related jobs such as field workers, accountants, engineers, trainers, secretaries, and others	Provides a picture of the entire strata of jobs	Must be very complete to show need for related occupations
Job survey	Determines whether and which programs are needed in a single occupation	Points to specific occupational needs; preliminary to curriculum development	Focuses on only one occupation; must survey across many employment settings
Employer survey	Determines local or regional employment needs; more in-depth than occupations survey because employers are asked to project needs	Provides trends; involves employers in planning	Projections may lack reliability and validity
Econometric studies	Conducted by the Bureau of Labor Statistics, U.S. Department of Labor, to determine ten-year employment needs on the basis of population, labor force, productivity, consumption, and overall output; estimates openings by occupation	More reliable than employer surveys; sophisticated methodology	Statistics are national, not always useful for regional or local projections; predictability based on economic forecasts for ten-year period
Job vacancy studies	Combines econometric studies with local or regional data to analyze present employment needs	Customizes data for regional purposes	Deals only with present needs; does not predict future needs
Trend extrapolation studies	Forecasts trends on basis of past trends	Inexpensive; quickly accomplished	Does not account for rapid change in the labor market; useful only for short-term predictions
Environmental scanning	Ongoing search for select information from a variety of sources to inform program development	Can provide the latest information on economic trends, labor markets, and political climates	Time consuming; can be expensive; care must be taken to ensure that proper categories for program development are scanned

absorb. A hypothetical example for a planned master's degree program in petroleum engineering illustrates the PNI analysis.

$$PNI = \frac{5{,}000 \text{ people employed as engineers in area}}{250 \text{ graduating master's degree engineers from area colleges}} = 20$$

Example for an undergraduate petroleum engineering program:

$$PNI = \frac{5{,}000 \text{ people employed as engineers in area}}{1{,}000 \text{ graduating bachelor's degree engineers from area schools}} = 5$$

In these examples the index value for the graduate petroleum engineering program is 20, while the value for the undergraduate program is 5, suggesting that the competitive position for the graduate degree program is considerably better. However, before resources are shifted to support the graduate program as a result of these formulas, more research is desirable. Perhaps further research would indicate that baccalaureate-level training in petroleum engineering is sufficient for entry into the field and that a graduate degree is superfluous for entrance.

It would be unwise to accept the results of the PNI applied to an institution's programs without first realizing its limitations. In these examples we first have to carefully determine what percentage of available jobs are accessible to candidates with a graduate degree before we can entertain weighty decisions about where to direct institutional resources. The mobility of job seekers trained at other institutions and willing to move into the geographic area of interest is also not factored by PNI analysis. It is also more difficult to apply data-driven techniques such as the PNI to liberal arts programs for the simple reason that relevant data are scarce, especially since no convenient, one-to-one correspondence exists between these programs and specific occupations.

To be relevant for a given institution, more information, primarily student follow-up data, is needed to determine what percentage of liberal arts graduates enter graduate school, find immediate employment, or elect to pursue studies in another field. For those students electing to extend their education, institutions will want to know the types of subject they are studying. Similarly, for those graduates who elect to work, institutions should know which employment fields they enter. More knowledge of the postgraduation experiences of all graduates, particularly liberal arts students, can point the way to modification of existing curricula or the need for new program development.

External Advisory Committees. External advisory committees are more common among two-year institutions. These groups, consisting of qualified professionals from the field that the new program is intended to address, can be invaluable in determining whether a new instructional program will be successful. Representatives from the private sector can act as a sounding board for employment needs and offer priceless insights into the curricular content of a proposed program. Formed on a standing basis to assist institutional decision makers, and when properly constructed with an eye to wide representation of employers within a specific employment market, such a committee can save the college from making a false start in launching a new program and can confirm or dispel data that an institution has collected to support program development. Later, after the program is launched, the committee can suggest benchmarks for program evaluation and make valuable employment leads available to program graduates. A program advisory committee is most successful when it has fresh, reliable data about a given program. Provision of such information is an important institutional research function.

Conclusions

Institutional research personnel should increase their involvement in instructional programming beyond the role required for program review and discontinuation. This chapter has presented techniques to assess the market potential for new programs, which institutional researchers can use to increase their involvement in this crucial component of institutional health. The need for institutions to demonstrate their connection to workforce development has been drawn even tighter during the recent economic downturn at the beginning of this century. Although some in academic circles will paint such activity as purely a vocational concern, it behooves institutions to be ready to answer where their programs align with the reality of the labor markets.

Accordingly, the most frequently used techniques presented in this chapter focus on employers and employment needs. The advantages and disadvantages of seven specific employer surveys and study techniques have been presented. The most popular of these techniques, the employer survey, promotes employer involvement in program development but may also lack validity and reliability. Other employment-related study techniques are more sophisticated but may be insensitive to rapid changes in labor markets. A survey of current students can produce invaluable insight for assessing market potential. Among the information institutions should collect from such a survey are preferences for scheduling classes, delivery mechanisms, perceptions of existing college services, and the need for specific programs.

Several commercially available surveys—especially the ESS, CIRP, SOIS, NSSE, and CCSSE—can furnish researchers with a convenient means of comparing marketing information for currently enrolled students with national profiles. These data can point to needed information on existing programs and services, to illuminate the processes of new program development. Though more difficult to obtain, similar data should also be collected for new target markets. As institutions expand into new markets, the preferences of prospective students for scheduling, program content, and institutional services must match the institution's ability to deliver.

Among other techniques reviewed in this chapter are values and lifestyles research and the Program Need Index. These techniques are new ways of approaching the fit between a proposed program and the market need for new and existing ones. Psychographic research in particular represents a departure from traditional demographic market research and is a fresh framework for matching programs with student characteristics.

Interest in program development appears to be on the rise as more institutions realize that change is unrelenting. This trend calls for an activist role for institutional research offices. During the initiation and preimplementation phases of program development, institutional personnel should forge alliances with personnel responsible for student recruitment, alteration in curricula, delivery systems, and student services. After a new program is implemented, immediate ties to other functional campus units can help the institutional research office evaluate its success. For the foreseeable future, public institutions will continue to face external pressure to eliminate nonproductive programs. This, in tandem with increased competition among institutions for students, constitutes an agenda that might appear to undercut institutional vitality. Against this backdrop, the techniques presented here for assessing the market potential of new programs merit serious consideration.

References

Environmental Systems Research Institute. "Community Tapestry Summary Segment Descriptions." Retrieved March 1, 2005, http://www.esribis.com/pdfs/ctsegments.pdf. 2004.

Kotler, P., and Fox, K. *Strategic Marketing for Educational Institutions.* Upper Saddle River, N.J.: Prentice Hall, 1995.

Nielsen, R. "Evaluating Market Opportunities for Academic Programs with a Program–Employment Opportunities–Competing Institutions Index." *College and University,* 1981, 56, 178–182.

Scientific Research International. *Understanding U.S. Consumers.* Menlo Park, Calif.: Scientific Research International, 2003.

Voorhees, R. A., and Hart, S. "Survey of Adult Preferences for College Classes and Services." Littleton, Colo.: Arapahoe Community College, 1985.

RICHARD A. VOORHEES *is principal of Voorhees Group LLC, an independent higher education consulting company in Littleton, Colorado.*

In this chapter, the authors argue that alignment of higher education with workforce needs should be based on careful action by institutions to embed skills and attributes within instructional programs.

Graduate Attributes and Their Development

Mantz Yorke, Lee Harvey

Twenty-five years ago, the majority of graduates in the UK and in many other Western countries went into the public sector (central and local government, education, and health services) or joined a large company, often on a fast-track graduate training scheme. This has changed as the number of graduates grows with the expansion of higher education. A majority of British graduates, for example, are now employed in small and medium-sized enterprises (SMEs). Large companies also recruit more graduates directly to jobs or as a result of taking students on work placement. The rapid pace of organizational and technological change and the need to respond to performance targets has meant that traditional graduate recruits no longer have the luxury of a leisurely training program. Graduates are increasingly expected to hit the ground running and make an impact quickly (a requirement that is particularly strong in SMEs, which do not have the capacity to provide the kind of training program available in a large organization).

This has meant that employers are growing increasingly demanding in recruiting graduates. Advertisements, Web sites, and recruitment literature are suggesting that graduates need to exhibit more and more attributes if they are going to be successful in the recruitment process. Having a degree is just the start, and employers nowadays seek a range of qualities and other achievements.

NEW DIRECTIONS FOR INSTITUTIONAL RESEARCH, no. 128, Winter 2005 © Lee Harvey. Printed with permission.

Skills and Abilities

Research over the last quarter of a century has shown a remarkable level of agreement in what employers want, despite each individual organization having its own specific requirements (Fergus, 1981; Caswell, 1983; Gordon, 1983; Wingrove and Herriot, 1984; Green, 1990; Harvey, Burrows, and Green, 1992; NBEET, 1992; Johnson and Pere-Vergé, 1993; British Telecom, 1993; Harvey and Green, 1994; Guirdham, 1995; Brennan, Kogan, and Teichler, 1996; Harvey, Moon, and Geall, 1997; Future Skills Wales, 1998; Conference Board of Canada, n.d.; Dunne, Bennett, and Carré, 2000). The core set of attributes has changed remarkably little, apart from a rise in information technology skills. Nonetheless, research has suggested that there are differences in views between manufacturing and service industries and government agencies, and that the size of the employer organization also has an impact on views. However, the evidence suggests that the requirements listed by employers are the overt tip of a much bigger iceberg of expectation.

Employers have always wanted a raft of other personal skills, not least adaptability, flexibility, and willingness to learn and continue learning. These have become increasingly important both for employers, who want a workforce that is able to respond to rapid change, and for graduates, who in many areas of work cannot expect a job for life and hence have to be responsive to opportunity.

Employers are less indulgent of graduates than they once were. Graduates need to be self-disciplined, tuned into organizational policy and culture, and able to work effectively with a range of other people. There has been a tendency, marked in private companies, toward a flatter management structure; much work is done in project teams, for which knowledge production is an interdisciplinary, rather than monodisciplinary, activity (Gibbons and others, 1994). Thus employers want graduates who are good communicators and team workers skilled in interpersonal behavior. Communication means writing in a variety of formats (producing formal reports, bullet-pointed summaries, and effective e-mails, for example), as well as being able to engage with clients, persuade colleagues in teams, and network within and outside the organization. Team working is not just about taking a specific role on a team but also being able to take different roles according to circumstances, and to work in several overlapping teams simultaneously. Time management and prioritizing of work are important capacities here. Interpersonal skills involve what has come to be known as "emotional intelligence" (Salovey and Mayer, 1990; Goleman, 1996), which includes appreciating the perspectives and concerns of others, understanding how to interact effectively in numerous settings, and being tactful and forceful when required.

Perhaps the biggest change over a quarter of a century has been the requirement to make effective use of communication and information technology. Graduates need to be accomplished at using information technology, have experience of a range of software, and be comfortable with using the various forms of electronic communication.

Employers have consistently emphasized the importance of problem solving (Harvey, Moon, and Geall, 1997). More recently, this has tended to become "creative problem solving," focusing on imaginative solutions, with employers looking for risk taking as part of the problem-solving strategy. However, it is not altogether clear how employers gauge the risk-taking potential of recruits. In passing, it should be noted that the desire to maintain a high grade point average or to obtain a "good honors degree" discourages risk taking during the study program.

Employers take on graduates because they want bright, intelligent people who will add value to what they are doing. In some cases (for example, medicine and engineering), the subject-specific knowledge and understanding that graduates have gained from their time in higher education is important. However, in a period of rapid advance in disciplinary knowledge, a grasp of underlying principles and the capacity to move one's repertoire of knowledge and understanding onward are vital.

There are many areas of employment in the UK in which a first degree in a specific subject is not necessary to follow a graduate-level career. For some students, then, degree-level study is more important as a vehicle for developing higher-level intellectual attributes of analysis, critical thinking, synthesis, and problem solving than it is for development of subject-specific expertise. Britain is probably at the forefront of nonsubject–specific recruitment (at least 50 percent of graduate recruitment is not subject-specific), but this trend is growing in Scandinavia and the United States. However, the practice is quite alien in some other parts of the world, notably India and most countries in eastern Asia.

The 1990s were characterized by approaches that sought to develop skills in both the United States and the UK. In the former, the Secretary's Commission on Achieving Necessary Skills was appointed by the secretary of labor to determine the skills needed to succeed in the world of work (SCANS, 1991). In the United Kingdom, "key skills" were first identified by the Confederation of British Industry and then relaunched by the Dearing Report (NCIHE, 1997). The Skills Task Force (1998), for example, claimed that "the lack of skills among graduates and young people is a key concern for employers." The Department for Education and Employment (DEE) Higher Education Projects Fund, 1998–2000, included projects funded to develop strategies to ensure all learners had the opportunity to develop key skills, employment skills, and transferable skills. As the projects developed, initial concern about the place of skills in the curriculum moved on to exploring the nature of a range of attributes, and where students might develop skills, how they might be assessed, and how skills link to the work environment (DEE, 2000).

Some employers have gone beyond compiling lists of desirable attributes to examine how these attributes enable graduates to be effective at work. The report *Graduates' Work* (Harvey, Moon, and Geall, 1997) is one of the few studies that moved from identifying attributes to exploring the relationship of attributes to roles that graduates will play in a flexible organization. The role the graduate plays varies with the setting, and it is important that he or she have the attributes to know when to fit into the workplace and do the job; when to take risks and persuade people of the merit of new ideas; and when to think laterally, take initiative and responsibility, and move the organization forward.

Robert Reich (1991, 2002) has been prominent in asserting the economic virtues of innovation and entrepreneurship. The argument is straightforward: when national policy emphasizes the importance of a knowledge-based economy, the need is to come up with new ideas and have the entrepreneurial skill to capitalize on them (failure to exploit innovations is often cited as a weakness in the UK economy). Higher education therefore has to feed these needs. However, Reich appears to undervalue the low-profile achievements that underpin economies and societies, such as success in providing services and in managing people and projects. If innovation and entrepreneurship are at the apex of the economic system, they can maintain that position only if they rest on a broad base of supportive activities, to which higher education makes a significant contribution, directly to enterprises and indirectly through programs addressing the social good.

Qualifications

This chapter concentrates on undergraduate degrees and qualifications at a lower level in higher education (two-year and four-year college equivalents in the U.S. system), rather than on postgraduate qualifications. Some bachelor's degrees are clearly vocation oriented (engineering, teacher education, and social work are three examples) whereas others are not (as examples, English, history, and sociology). Yet even if a degree program is not directly vocational, it is still likely to develop in a student capabilities that are entirely relevant to the work situation: critical analysis, problem solving, team working, and presentation skills.. There are two important matters for the labor market. First, curricula should demonstrate an awareness of the needs of the labor market. Second, students should be aware of their achievements and how they might relate to employers' needs. The first is being addressed in the UK through expectations imposed on higher education institutions by funding bodies; regarding the second, there is some evidence that students' awareness and representation of their achievements could be improved.

The "employability debate" in the UK has tended to concentrate on students who enter higher education directly from school or further education college. Relatively little attention is given to those who enter higher education as "mature students," but such students are likely to bring with them considerable experience as an employee and as a person who has exercised responsibility for others (dependents, for example). Much that goes under the label of employability will have already been achieved by such people. Their developmental needs may lie more in developing self-confidence in the academic sphere than in relating to the broader life-world.

Foundation and other predegree programs (two-year U.S. equivalents) are, in some instances, more closely attuned to the labor market than a degree program (four-year program). Robertson (2002) identifies a series of characteristics of predegree higher education programs that are present in national systems to a varying extent:

In comparison with degrees, they have been designed with an eye to the local labor market.
Where they do meet local (or regional) labor market needs, they tend to recruit well.
They contain work placement or other form of work experience.
They are trusted by employers.
They are cost-efficient compared with on-the-job training.

Over the years, higher education institutions in the UK have offered a "sandwich degree" (analogous to cooperative education programs in the United States, Canada, and Ireland and internships in parts of Europe) in which one or more periods of work experience are interspersed in the academic curriculum (see Chapter Two). They have been vulnerable to the vicissitudes of the economy, and in a period of recession have been replaced by programs without a work-experience component; in the UK, business studies was an area badly affected in this way in the late 1980s. Government policy in England favors work experience for as many higher education students as possible, but since this policy extends to the later years of schooling the pressure on organizations for places may prove too great to satisfy demand.

In 2000, the foundation degree was launched in England, Wales, and Northern Ireland; it is currently running in parallel with the longer-established Higher National Diploma (HND, a two-year full-time program with a vocational emphasis) and its part-time equivalent, the Higher National Certificate or HNC, designed for those typically in full-time employment (Table 4.1). Scotland has broadly analogous HND and HNC programs but has not opted to run foundation degrees.

Foundation degree programs feature employer involvement, development of skills and knowledge, application of skills in the workplace, credit accumulation and transfer, and progression (within work or to an honors degree). But what differentiates them from HNDs (and, to a lesser extent, HNCs) is that they incorporate a substantial proportion of work-based learning. In the first two years of existence, the foundation degree showed greatest participation by people who are at work but seeking to upgrade their qualifications, rather than by students opting for the full-time, two-year route.

Table 4.1. UK Predegree and Degree Qualification Structure (and U.S. Equivalents)

	HND (Full-Time)	HNC (Part-Time)	Foundation Degree	Bachelor's Degree*	Sandwich Degree	U.S. Two-Year Associate	U.S. Four-Year Bachelor's
Year 1	✓	✓		✓	✓	✓	✓
Year 2	Qualification (transfer to degree is possible but often to repeat second year)	✓	Qualification or transfer to third year of degree	✓	✓	Qualification or transfer to degree	✓
Year 3		Qualification		Three-year qualification B.A./B.Sc.	Year in work placement	✓	✓
Year 4					Four-year qualification B.A./B.Sc.		Four-year qualification B.A./B.Sc.

Note: * Medical, dentistry, and veterinary degrees take five or more years of full-time study.

In the United States, there is a strong tradition of two-year programs in community colleges and other specialist institutions that lead to the associate degree, which can subsequently be "topped up" to a bachelor's award at a four-year institution (however, a survey by VanDerLinden, 2002, suggests that around 80 percent of all community college students will stick with the associate degree and not seek to transfer to a baccalaureate program). The associate degree is valued by employers; it is predominantly linked with the local economy, and enrollment has fluctuated over the years with the state of the national economy (Cohen and Brawer, 1996). There appears to have been some narrowing of the salary differential with those holding a four-year degree. In a country in which tuition fees are a serious consideration, the relative cheapness of the associate degree compared to the full degree has its attraction.

In Germany, there is a stronger commitment to vocational programs than is found in the UK. The German *Fachhochschulen* offer vocational programs that are short in comparison to degree programs and allow entry to students with qualifications that are lower than those needed for entry to a degree program. However, they tend not to lead on to university study because the qualifications do not tie in with university expectations regarding entry for a degree program.

In France, the *diplôme d'études universitaires générales* (DEUG) and *diplôme d'études universitaires scientifiques et techniques* (DEUST) are viewed as "first-cycle" programs, with the license (the equivalent of a bachelor's degree) forming the second cycle. The DEUG and DEUST are predominantly used as entry qualifications for the license. They have limited value as entry qualifications for the labor market, although Robertson (2002) reports that more than 40 percent of students on DEUG and license programs (the data are undifferentiated) undertake a work placement. On the other hand, the two-year *diplôme universitaire de technologie* (DUT, covering technology, engineering, and related subjects) is more related to the labor market; it involves a ten-week period of work experience and is in part staffed by work-based professionals. The *brevet de technicien supérieur* (BTS) is an employment-oriented technician qualification also involving work experience, enrollment for which has, despite the lower prestige, grown by the greatest amount during the last two decades. The *diplôme d'université* (DU), with two- and four-year variants, is perhaps the closest to the vocationally oriented associate degree in the United States, in that it is a program developed through collaboration between a university and its local industry. Elsewhere in Europe, subbaccalaureate programs act more as a filter for degree programs than as a terminal qualification.

The Contribution of Theory

Preparing graduates for the labor market has been a strongly pragmatic activity. Higher education makes itself aware of the needs of employers through a range of sources, among them professional bodies, employers' organizations, and institution-based liaison committees with employer members. Higher education has tended to overlook the extent to which the knowledge it has generated might contribute to curriculum design for what in the UK is termed employability (this term has yet to gain global currency, although it is becoming significant in the European Union; Yorke, 2004).

One way of linking employability definitions (see Chapter Two) to theory is through the "USEM" account of employability, which is applicable to vocational and nonvocational programs alike:

- Understanding of the subject discipline, and of matters pertinent to performance in an organization.
- Skillful practices in context, with respect to both the subject discipline and an organization. (Interpreting skills in this way avoids the narrowness of "skill and drill" and acknowledges the "situatedness" of cognition that has been highlighted by writers such as Lave and Wenger, 1991; Wenger, 1998; and Brown and Duguid, 2000. This is particularly important in the UK, where for a decade and a half governments have pressed an atheoretical "skills agenda" on the education system.)
- Efficacy beliefs, a term sweeping up a range of personal qualities and attributes that have a bearing on the chances of a graduate being effective in work and social life.
- Metacognition, in which reflective practice (following Schön, 1983, and others) and self-regulation are prominent.

Bennett, Dunne, and Carré (2000) offer a theoretical perspective based on a person's performance; however, the individual psychological conditions that *underpin* the person's performance are given little emphasis.

The interrelationships among the four USEM components and employability are shown in Figure 4.1.

The USEM account, with just four components contributing to employability, allows academics to interpret it with reference to the norms and expectations relevant to their particular discipline. It therefore allows them to exercise their professional judgment and avoids straitjacketing. In the European Union, this interpretability is termed *subsidarity;* a concern is, however, that the permissiveness inherent in subsidarity might lead to an unacceptable level of divergence. When presented with USEM and hearing a strong connection being made with good learning, academics find the approach much more satisfying than one to employability that is based on relatively narrow interpretation of core skills, key skills, and so on, even though some may not like the all-encompassing nature (and perhaps the label) of "efficacy beliefs" and the semijargon of "metacognition." However, there is an appreciation that USEM rests on theory and empirical research in a way that has not been the case with promotion of skills in the UK. A full response to USEM raises curricular challenges, however, especially in respect to modular curricula. This substantial issue is addressed later.

Figure 4.1. Schematic Representation of the USEM Account of Employability

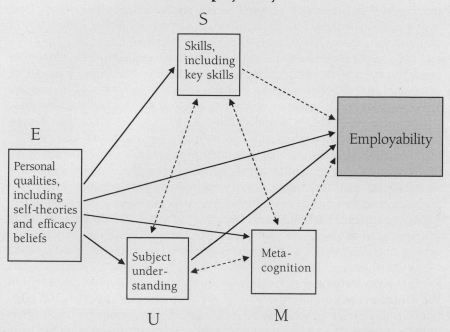

Note: E (efficacy beliefs) demonstrates pervasive importance

USEM posits, in a broad sense, the kind of achievement that employers say they value. However, the E and M, and some aspects of skillful practices, resist summative grading. Although students can make claims to achievement (for example, via a portfolio), the claims are more difficult for employers to weigh when faced with a pile of applications; the apparent certitude of a GPA or degree classification, interpreted with reference to the institution from which the qualification was gained, has an obvious attraction. If employers are to take seriously the implications of a USEM-type of approach to employability, then a corollary is that they will need to acknowledge that simple "measures" can tell only a limited part of the graduate's achievement. A role for institutional researchers would be to analyze the extent to which embedding of employability in the curriculum is based on a theoretical model and to what extent it reproduces predetermined skills lists.

The "Fit" of USEM with Graduate Success in the UK. The development of USEM is too recent for curricula to have been designed with it as an underpinning approach. Hence it is possible only to retrofit graduate experiences in organizations to the approach, and in doing so it is possible to demonstrate a plausible, but not definitive, connection with the constructs embedded in USEM. Some recent research, along with certain established studies, show a good degree of fit between the USEM model and the requirements and desires of employers and recent graduate recruits.

A series of interviews were conducted, as part of the Skills Plus project (Knight and Yorke, 2004), with 97 recently recruited graduate employees and 117 of their more senior colleagues. The latter tended to be in close contact with the new recruits, rather than people with high-level managerial responsibilities, on the argument that the project was interested in employability as it was understood by recent recruits and those with relatively close contact with them. This is "employability on the ground" rather than as seen from the more rarefied perspective of the human resource manager.

The recently recruited were asked about the factors that had been influential in their gaining employment, whereas their senior colleagues were asked about what they thought was important in new recruits. The broad picture presented by the two respondent groups shows a close similarity regarding what they felt had been important (Table 4.2), though there were differences of emphasis and detail at a finer level of analysis. This is quite similar to the responses from similar groups in the Graduates' Work study (Harvey, Moon, and Geall, 1997).

Efficacy Beliefs. Personal qualities featured particularly strongly in the comments of both groups. The 97 recent recruits mentioned 108 attributes in this category, whereas their colleagues made more than 550 references to personal qualities of various kinds. Some critical comments from the senior colleagues focused on the lack of attention in higher education to the development of practical, work-related skills and appropriate personal qualities; communication with, and working with, others were prominent. However, there were differences in emphasis according to the employment sector. The industrial sector tended to emphasize proactivity, self-drivenness, and the capacity to cope with pressure, whereas the health and social services sector tended (not surprisingly) to highlight self-awareness, empathy, concern for people, helpfulness, and approachability. Personal qualities therefore seem to weigh heavily in construing employability. This is also consistent with the findings of Harvey, Moon, and Geall (1997).

Communication ability was widely mentioned as important. This goes beyond the construction of essay-type answers to assignments and examination questions to include the skills of summarizing, extracting key points, presenting to others in various situations and using appropriate media, and making effective use of the Internet and the Web. In a work environment, employees rarely have time to conduct the kind of exhaustive research that is deemed desirable for an academic assignment; they typically have to work with incomplete information and to a tight deadline, with experience and judgment filling in the gaps. Communication takes the form of the best that can be done in such circumstances, rather than something closer to perfection.

Concern about poor communication seems common to both the United States and the UK. Current work sponsored by RAND is exploring

Table 4.2. Main Features of Employability as Reported by Recently Recruited Graduates and Their More Senior Colleagues

Recently Recruited Graduates	More Senior Colleagues
• Personal qualities	• Personal characteristics
• Communication skills	• Communication skills
• Degree experience	• Quality of, and performance in, education
• Work experience	• Work experience

use of a broad cognitive test that requires students to demonstrate critical thinking, analytic reasoning, and written communication. This research reflects concerns expressed in reports by the National Center for Public Policy and Higher Education (NCPPHE, 2000, 2002) and some major employers (Roger Benjamin, personal communication, 2004) that graduating students have insufficiently developed capacities such as these.

Understanding and Skillful Practices in Context. For both groups of respondents, the degree experience was important, as would be expected. This was a matter of developing not only expertise in the subject discipline but also the more generic achievements that have value in employment and the wider society: the "skillful practices in context" reflecting the situatedness of learning noted earlier. A few recent recruits regretted that their degree experience had not helped them to acquire some of the understanding that is tacit in the way that organizations conduct their affairs (or, in Sternberg's terms, to develop the "practical intelligence" that aids success; Sternberg, 1997). How academe operates was felt, by a few, not to have helped them develop skills in time management, prioritizing of work, and working with others—a view frequently voiced in the Graduates' Work study (Harvey, Moon, and Geall, 1997) as well. For the senior colleagues, weight tended to be placed in varying proportion on a combination of the graduate's academic performance and the reputation of the institution at which the person had studied. However, the classification of the degree was not necessarily the most important thing.

A danger noted by one senior respondent was that "good workers" might get weeded out during the selection process while academic high fliers progressed (with academic intelligence perhaps being privileged over practical intelligence). Recent proposals by eight top law schools in the UK to introduce an additional selection examination indicate the ongoing tension between the academic and the practical, as Berlins sharply pointed out: "Very many successful lawyers—I say this in praise, not criticism—are not all that bright. Some of our best judges do not shine intellectually. Becoming a good lawyer requires a mixture of talents, of which the intelligence revealed by the proposed tests is only one. Equally, many bright people have proved to be rubbish lawyers. Put bluntly, many of our best lawyers and judges would have failed these tests, and we would have been the poorer without them. And many potentially excellent lawyers will be lost to the law because of these tests" (2004, p. 17).

Recent recruits and their more senior colleagues testified to the value of work experience (Table 4.1). This can take many forms, ranging from placements up to a year (as in formal cooperative education programs) down to relatively casual part-time employment outside the program (as is undertaken widely in the United States, the UK, and Australia; see Chapter Two). The importance of understanding that, as one senior colleague put it, "commonsense real life isn't as in the textbooks" was acknowledged by a number of the recently recruited graduates. Their comments included the following examples, which reflect Bereiter and Scardamalia's perspective (1993) on the development of expertise through blending academic and practical understandings.

The value of learning from any form of work or voluntary experience was stressed in a number of interviews. The comment of a senior employer illustrates the point: "We would expect everybody to have had some sort of work experience, even if it's holiday working, part-time working . . . just any working environment where they've had to work with people, understand some of the politics that goes on, and maybe see if they understand any of the financial aspects as well."

The value of work experience came through so strongly in the 258 in-depth interviews with employers and recent graduates in the Graduates' Work study (Harvey, Moon, and Geall, 1997) that it became a central recommendation of the National Committee of Inquiry into Higher Education report (NCIHE, 1997), highlighted on the front page of the *Times*. The concern, however, is sometimes expressed that part-time employment (in contrast to a placement that is part of the curriculum or co-curriculum) adversely affects students' academic performance. The evidence, though, is not clear-cut. Pascarella and Terenzini (1991) suggest that part-time employment can be beneficial if undertaken on campus, but (as Astin, 1993, also reports) not if off campus. Stinebrickner and Stinebrickner (n.d.) found a negative effect of part-time working on academic performance, though this was from a single college in Kentucky with a relatively disadvantaged student profile. Lundberg (2003) indicates that the advantages and disadvantages are not consistent across the spectrum of students. There is ambivalent evidence from a relatively limited study conducted in one university in England (Barke and others, 2000). This has to be set against the collateral benefit of the more generic kind of learning that can accrue from experience in workplaces and voluntary service but that is less easy to quantify. Results from student surveys suggest there is considerable variation in views about the perceived benefits and deficits of part-time work while undertaking a full-time degree program.

Metacognition. Reflection is often put forward as a desirable characteristic of a graduate, though it figured only to a limited extent in the Skills Plus interviews. One senior employee expected a capacity for reflection to have been developed in the degree program: "If someone . . . said they'd got a degree . . . I would expect them to have . . . been doing certain things that would make them aware of . . . the way they think. . . ."

Another expected this to be connected with the self-confidence to decide whether a matter could be handled alone or whether the support of a senior colleague might be needed: "We are looking about them having some insight as to when you might need to talk to your manager, when you might need to talk to your colleagues or when you can be expected to resolve those issues yourself. . . ."

Rarely did a junior interviewee discuss things that could be subsumed under metacognition. One of the exceptions realized that she needed to take a counseling course to better empathize and communicate with people, and another undertook a SWOT (strengths, weaknesses, opportunities, and threats) analysis on her own initiative "just because I felt I needed to do it, not because it was part of my training." Metacognition includes people's awareness that they need to continue their learning and cannot rely on what they have gained from their formal studies.

It can be seen, then, that the USEM model provides a framework for appraising and revising curricula.

Some Curricular Implications

Employability is a slow-growing crop. The development of understanding, of skillful practice, of metacognition, and of the self is characterized by "slow learning" (Claxton, 1998) and requires repetition of broadly similar, yet progressive, learning experiences if it is to be fully successful. Employability is a manifestation of complex learning; hence it is not well served by the gesture of incorporating into the program a separate module on skills development (or similar), since that is likely to lead to the complex being treated as if simple. The fragmentation of curricula also ghettoizes employability.

There is a question as to whether self-efficacy can be developed through higher education (or be taught without the teacher having to become an expert in psychology). The need is for the teacher to be aware of how students, some of whom may be unsure of their "right" to be in higher education, can be encouraged and discouraged. The teacher does not have to be a quasi-psychologist, just a thoughtful and informed teacher who makes judicious use of formative assessment, seeking to build students' capacities rather than emphasize their weaknesses (Knight and Yorke, 2003; Yorke and Knight, 2004).

In the UK, as in the United States and elsewhere, there has been a move toward defining expected learning outcomes of programs: stating what students are expected to be able to *do* at the end of the study units and of the program as a whole. This is of uncontestable importance, but the shift in curricular emphasis has distracted attention from important processual matters, including development of students' personal qualities and attributes that are important as "enablers" of learning as well as outcomes of significance to the world outside academe. Dweck (1999), Pintrich (2000), and Sternberg (1997) are among writers who have discussed the "developability" of intelligence; likewise Bandura (1997) on self-efficacy, with Sternberg and Grigorenko (2000) suggesting that practical intelligence is likely to be progressively augmented over time whereas academic intelligence may decline gently from early adulthood. The desirability of developing students as persons emphasizes the need for curricula attention to the E in USEM.

Program Level. Where curricula are modular (unitized), the modules are likely to be relatively freestanding despite their content being logically and epistemologically connected. This poses a challenge for student development that extends beyond modular boundaries, since coherence and progression of learning experience requires program-level commitment. In practice, it may often be unrealistic to expect a complete curriculum to address a pervasive theme such as employability (though Alverno College has demonstrated the feasibility of a programwide commitment to overarching principles), and hence it may be wiser to concentrate attention on those modules that form the core of the program.

Without going to the extent of redesigning core curricula, a lot can be done by analyzing the spread of activities across modules in the core curriculum, looking for duplication (for example, students having to give presentations; Mason, Williams, Cranmer, and Guile, 2003; or to write essays in most of their modules); absence of expectations that might have been laid down at the program level; and discontinuities in the progression of activities (for example, not explicitly developing the skills that are needed for a later module). Analyses of this sort can assist a program team to improve development of students' employability.

Assessment and Recognition of Achievement. It is widely understood that the assessment régime for a program influences students' behavior. Students, reasonably enough, attend to what they see as counting toward their GPA or award. This is a rational and strategic approach to assessment, seeking the best return on the effort put in. In the UK, a so-called good degree is the basic entry ticket to a range of opportunities, from research studentship to employment in a company that attracts a large number of applicants for posts.

Although assessment of achievement in the subject discipline is not generally considered to be problematic, assessment of other achievements that are of significance for employment is much more challenging. These are sometimes referred to as "soft skills." Among them are the ability to work effectively in teams, empathize with clients and customers, and demonstrate creativity—three of many examples of achievement that are difficult to capture in a grading system. Knight and Yorke (2003) argue that if employability is to be treated seriously, the need is for an assessment régime that can pick up those achievements that resist grading. The softer kinds of achievement (such as the three just noted) could perhaps be graded if sufficient time and resources were available, but in practice this turns out to be an unrealistic ideal. Hence the need is for an alternative approach that can do justice to the full spectrum of achievement.

Student construction of a portfolio of achievement offers a way forward, since this can furnish the evidence base from which a graduate can construct justification of why he or she should be considered for a job. The portfolio will contain records of achievement in the subject discipline that are couched in traditional terms (grade point or percentage, for example), transcripts indicating the modules that have been studied, and evidence of achievement from outside the subject discipline (such as success in program-relevant work experience, other work experience, volunteering, and life in general; see Chapter Two for details).

The move away from the traditional representation of a graduate's achievement to an approach based on a broad portfolio of achievements does not undermine the value and validity of a high level of performance within a subject discipline. The portfolio-based approach can be regarded as a "yes, and . . . " way of representing achievement rather than one characterized as "no, but. . . ." How might it be received by employers? The first reaction might be negative, on the grounds that a relatively simple criterion (GPA or degree class) for sifting applications would be partially obscured; the employer would be required to dig for the relevant information. A more considered response might be to say that, despite the greater effort needed at the initial sifting stage, there would be a benefit in having a fuller picture of what an applicant has to offer. After all, recruiting an employee is an investment decision that demands attention to both benefits and costs.

There has, for some time, been a concern in the UK that student achievement is represented less than ideally by the honors degree classification system. The problem is to find an approach that can convey with greater richness what a graduate has to offer. The employers' perspective will be influential in determining the direction that representation of student achievement should take. It remains to be seen whether their commitment to employability (as outlined in this chapter) is a rhetorical flourish or something considerably deeper.

The importance of assessment in situating employability is another important research task for institutional researchers, namely, auditing and analyzing approaches adopted to assess employability skills, abilities, and attitudes. What is done to formatively and summatively assess attributes, and what degree of importance is placed on them in summative assessment?

References

Astin, A. *What Matters in College? Four Critical Years Revisited.* San Francisco: Jossey-Bass, 1993.

Bandura, A. *Self-Efficacy: The Exercise of Control.* New York: Freeman, 1997.

Barke, M., Braidford, P., Houston, M., Hunt, A., Lincoln, I., Morphet, C., Stone, I., and Walker, A. "Students in the Labour Market: Nature, Extent and Implications of Term-Time Employment Among University of Northumbria Undergraduates." Research Report 215. London: Department for Education and Skills, 2000.

Bennett, N., Dunne, E., and Carré, R. *Skills Development in Higher Education and Employment.* Buckingham, England: SRHE and the Open University Press, 2000.

Bereiter, C., and Scardamalia, M. *Surpassing Ourselves: An Inquiry into the Nature and Implications of Expertise.* Chicago: Open Court, 1993.

Berlins, M. "Janet Jackson's Right Breast Could Hurt Millions—in the Pocket, If Nowhere Else." *Guardian G2 Supplement,* Feb. 10, 2004, p. 17.

Brennan, J., Kogan, M., and Teichler, U. (eds.). *Higher Education and Work.* London: Jessica Kingsley, 1996.

British Telecom. *Matching Skills: A Question of Demand and Supply.* London: British Telecom, 1993.

Brown, J. S., and Duguid, P. *The Social Life of Information.* Cambridge Mass.: Harvard University Press, 2000.

Caswell, P. "Graduate Recruits: What Do Employers Look for?" *Teaching News,* Mar. 18, 1983, pp. 13–15.

Claxton, G. *Hare Brain, Tortoise Mind.* London: Fourth Estate, 1998.

Cohen, A. M., and Brawer, F. B. *The American Community College.* (3rd ed.) San Francisco: Jossey-Bass, 1996.

Conference Board of Canada. "Employability Skills 2000+." Retrieved July 28, 2005, http://www.conferenceboard.ca/education/learning-tools/pdfs/esp2000.pdf. n.d.

Department for Education and Employment (DEE). "Higher Education Digest, Special Issue" (on Higher Education Development Projects). Retrieved July 28, 2005, http://www.dfes.gov.uk/dfee/heqe/cheri_dfee_digest.pdf. 2000.

Dunne, E., Bennett, N., and Carré, C. "Skill Development in Higher Education and Employment." In F. Coffield (ed.), *Differing Visions of a Learning Society: Research Findings, Vol. I.* Bristol, England: Policy Press and ESRC, 2000.

Dweck, C. S. *Self-Theories: Their Role in Motivation, Personality, and Development.* Philadelphia: Psychology Press, 1999.

Fergus, A. "Selecting New Graduates for Administration and Management." *BACIE Journal,* 1981, *36*(1), 19–21.

Future Skills Wales. "A Report Addressing the Future Skill Needs of Wales, 1998–2007: Main Report for All Wales" by MORI Research and Business Strategies. Cardiff, UK: Welsh Development Agency, 1998.

Gibbons, M., Limoges, C., Nowotny, H., Schwartzman, S., Scott, P., and Trow, M. *The New Production of Knowledge: The Dynamics of Science and Research in Contemporary Societies.* London: Sage, 1994.

Goleman, D. *Emotional Intelligence.* London: Bloomsbury, 1996.

Gordon, A. "Attitudes of Employers to the Recruitment of Graduates." *Educational Studies,* 1983, *9*(1), 45–64.

Green, S. "Analysis of Transferable Personal Skills Requested by Employers in Graduate Recruitment Advertisements in June 1989." Sheffield, England: University of Sheffield, 1990.

Guirdham, M. *Interpersonal Skills at Work.* (2nd ed.) Upper Saddle River, N.J.: Prentice Hall, 1995.

Harvey, L., Burrows, A., and Green, D. "Someone Who Can Make an Impression: Report of the Employers' Survey of Qualities of Higher Education Graduates." Birmingham, England: QHE, 1992.

Harvey, L., and Green, D. "Employer Satisfaction." Birmingham, England: Quality in Higher Education, University of Central England, 1994.

Harvey, L., Moon, S., and Geall, V., with Bower, R. "Graduates' Work: Organization Change and Students' Attributes." Birmingham, England: Centre for Research into Quality (CRQ) and Association of Graduate Recruiters (AGR), 1997.

Johnson, D., and Pere-Vergé, L. "Attitudes Towards Graduate Employment in the SME Sector." *International Small Business Journal,* 1993, *11*(4), 65–70.

Knight, P. T., and Yorke, M. *Assessment, Learning and Employability.* Maidenhead, England: SRHE and Open University Press, 2003.

Knight, P., and Yorke, M. *Learning, Curriculum and Employability in Higher Education.* London: Routledge Falmer, 2004.

Lave, J., and Wenger, E. *Situated Learning: Legitimate Peripheral Participation.* Cambridge, England: Cambridge University Press, 1991.

Lundberg, C. A. "The Influence of Time-Limitations, Faculty and Peer Relationships on Adult Student Learning: A Causal Model." *Journal of Higher Education,* 2003, *74*(6), 665–688.

Mason, G., Williams, G., Cranmer, S., and Guile, D. "How Much Does Higher Education Enhance the Employability of Graduates?" Retrieved July 28, 2005, http://www.hefce.ac.uk/Pubs/RDreports/2003/rd13_03/. 2003.

National Board of Employment, Education, and Training (NBEET). *Skills Required of Graduates: One Test of Quality in Australian Higher Education.* Canberra: Australian Government Publishing Service, 1992.

National Center for Public Policy and Higher Education. "Measuring up 2000: The State-by-State Report Card for Higher Education." Retrieved July 28, 2005, http://measuringup.highereducation.org/2000/. 2000.

National Center for Public Policy and Higher Education. "Measuring up 2002: The State-by-State Report Card for Higher Education." Retrieved July 28, 2005, http://measuringup.highereducation.org/2002/reporthome.htm. 2002.

National Committee of Inquiry into Higher Education (NCIHE). *Higher Education in the Learning Society.* London: Her Majesty's Stationery Office, 1997.

Pascarella, E. T., and Terenzini, P. T. *How College Affects Students.* San Francisco: Jossey-Bass, 1991.

Pintrich, P. R. "The Role of Goal Orientation in Self-Regulated Learning." In M. Boekaerts, P. Pintrich, and M. Zeidner (eds.), *Handbook of Self-Regulation.* New York: Academic Press, 2000.

Reich, R. B. *The Work of Nations.* London: Simon and Schuster, 1991.

Reich, R. B. *The Future of Success.* London: Vintage, 2002.

Robertson, D. "Intermediate-Level Qualifications in Higher Education: An International Assessment." Retrieved July 28, 2005, http://www.hefce.ac.uk/pubs/rdreports/2002/rd10_02/. 2002.

Salovey, P., and Mayer, J. D. "Emotional Intelligence." *Imagination, Cognition, and Personality,* 1990, *9,* 185–211.

Schön, D. *The Reflective Practitioner: How Professionals Think in Action.* New York: Basic Books, 1983.

Secretary's Commission on Achieving Necessary Skills (SCANS). *What Work Requires of Schools.* Springfield, Va.: National Technical Information Service (NTIS), Technology Administration, U.S. Department of Commerce, 1991.

Skills Task Force. *Towards a National Skills Agenda: First Report of the National Skills Task Force.* Sudbury, Suffolk, England: Prolog, 1998.

Sternberg, R. J. *Successful Intelligence: How Practical and Creative Intelligence Determine Success in Life.* New York: Plume, 1997.

Sternberg, R. J., and Grigorenko, E. L. "Practical Intelligence and Its Development." In R. Bar-On and J. Parker (eds.), *The Handbook of Emotional Intelligence.* San Francisco: Jossey-Bass, 2000.

Stinebrickner, T. R., and Stinebrickner, R. "Working During School and Academic Performance." Retrieved July 28, 2005, http://www.ssc.uwo.ca/economics/econref/html/WP2000/wp2000_9.pdf. n.d.

VanDerLinden, K. *Credit Student Analysis: 1999 and 2000.* In *Faces of the Future: A Portrait of America's Community College Students* (survey report). Annapolis Junction, Md.: Community College Press, 2002.

Wenger, E. *Communities of Practice: Learning, Meaning and Identity.* Cambridge, England: Cambridge University Press, 1998.

Wingrove, J., and Herriot, P. "Graduate Pre-Selection: Some Findings and Their Guidance Implications." *British Journal of Guidance Counselling,* 1984, *12*(2), 166–174.

Yorke, M. "Employability in Higher Education: What It Is, What It Is Not." York, England: Learning and Teaching Support Network. Retrieved July 28, 2005, www.heacademy.ac.uk/resources.asp?process=full_record&section=generic&id=336. 2004.

Yorke, M., and Knight, P. T. "Self-Theories: Some Implications for Teaching and Learning in Higher Education." *Studies in Higher Education,* 2004, *29*(1), 25–37.

MANTZ YORKE *is director of the Centre for Higher Education Development at Liverpool John Moores University, United Kingdom.*

LEE HARVEY *is professor and director of the Centre for Research and Evaluation at Sheffield Hallam University, United Kingdom.*

5

*Accountability and reporting mechanisms go hand in
hand with government programs that promote workforce
development. This chapter describes current practice in
the United States and suggests how institutional
researchers can help improve the process of documenting
outcomes.*

Accountability Measures in Workforce Training

Kent A. Phillippe

On its surface, the Tenth Amendment to the U.S. Constitution ("The powers not delegated to the United States by the Constitution, nor prohibited by it to the states, are reserved to the states respectively, or to the people") may appear to have little relevance to accountability in workforce training programs. It has, however, a significant impact on how legislation related to assessment and measurement of workforce training outcomes is implemented. There is long-standing tension between the federal and state governments over the responsibility for workforce training and how outcomes of that training should be measured. The United States, unlike other Western countries, has never had a centralized, national entity to oversee education and training. As a result, many provisions of federal law allow individual states to develop plans for providing training and measuring the outcomes of that training.

The federal resources for workforce development flow from two separate, but linked, pieces of legislation, the Carl D. Perkins Vocational and Applied Technology Education Act (as amended in 1998, Public Law 105–332, and referred to as Perkins III) and the Workforce Investment Act (WIA) of 1998 (Public Law 105–220). The former offers resources for career and technical training to states that in turn allocate funds by formula to secondary and postsecondary schools. The latter is a continuation of federal "second chance" alternatives for workers and employers that furnishes services mainly through One-Stop Centers. The WIA is an attempt to streamline and consolidate a mishmash of government efforts for the unemployed into one program that would give job seekers more opportunities to pursue career training. In 1998, Congress briefly considered consolidating these two laws to integrate postsecondary education into state and local systems for workforce development and job training. Instead, Congress opted for coordination between the two, including coordinated accountability. However, as demonstrated in this chapter, their performance indicators are largely unsynchronized.

WIA replaced federal statutes governing job training, adult education and literacy, and vocational rehabilitation with a national system that was more streamlined and recognizable. Its principal predecessor, the Job Training Partnership Act, was noteworthy because it relegated oversight responsibility to the states and created private industry councils (PICs) to oversee regional training and employer needs. PICs used community colleges as well as a range of nonprofit and community-based training providers to make services available. WIA continues this tradition by pushing accountability decisions downward to the point of service and by giving state and local government the primary responsibility to implement and oversee all programs.

WIA legislation replaced the system of PICs with local workforce investment boards (WIBs) charged with developing the five-year local workforce investment plan, selecting One-Stop Career Center operators, maintaining employment-related services, and appointing a youth council. One-Stop operators were charged with administering a system of individual training accounts (vouchers) to pay for training of eligible workers by those training providers certified by WIBs. The list of eligible training providers may or may not include regionally accredited institutions of higher education, and the decision as to whom to include as service providers is largely decided by state officials.

Perkins III continued a tradition of furnishing resources to states for career and technical education. Perkins III is also unique in its approach, because it specifically indicates that postsecondary funds be used at community colleges, rather than traditional four-year colleges. Perkins III also increases the states' role in developing performance indicators. Among other provisions, Perkins III requires that vocational students be held to the same academic standards as other students and directs more resources to local programs rather than to statewide administration. Its higher-stakes accountability provisions were revolutionary, at least in higher education, as, for the first time, providers were required to report outcome data to a central state administrative agency that in turn aggregates these data and reports them to the U.S. Department of Education. Both laws introduced potential rewards and consequences for states that do or do not improve student performance; states that exceed their agreed-on level of performance under both WIA and Perkins III are eligible for incentive funding.

Perkins III and WIA authorized appropriation of federal funds through September 30, 2003. As of this writing, the authority for both programs has been extended pending Congressional reauthorization. Several proposals have been made to maintain both programs separately as well as to consolidate them. It is too early to predict which changes either program (or both) might make in accountability mandates, although current proposals use many of the same performance indicators in current legislation, these are to be explicated shortly. Many of these performance indicators are viewed by community colleges as inadequate to capture the various successful outcomes possible for postsecondary students. Still other proposals point to the usefulness of combining—not simply both laws—but certain of their performance indicators as well. Whatever changes are forthcoming, however, it is certain that the model of centralized state reporting to the federal government will be preserved.

At the same time that the United States has moved toward a more centralized method of collecting and reporting accountability, in some other nations the opposite is true. Denmark is a good example, having chosen to move the accountability out to the individual institutions: "By decentralisation measures and a more withdrawn role of the government the colleges have acquired much more autonomy. This has led to an enhanced interest by the government towards quality care measures as a way to secure the efficient and qualified 'production' of colleges in a new setting where the traditional detailed steering principles have been abandoned" (Manning and Lasonen, 2005).

Another example is the European Union's Leonardo da Vinci Community Vocational Training Action Program. The program actively supports the lifelong training policies conducted by the member states. It supports transnational initiatives for promoting the knowledge, aptitudes, and skills necessary for successful integration into working life and full exercise of citizenship, and it affords scope for links with other community initiatives—particularly the Socrates and Youth programs—by supporting joint action. The accountability measures are left to the program implementers and monitored by the "national agency or commission" associated with the program. As in the United States, however, there are no consistent measures across the programs (European Commission, n.d.).

Despite the incongruence that plagues outcome measures in both U.S. laws, recent history has demonstrated the federal government's interest in uniform measures across all programs. However, historical practices within states make this goal neither easy nor practical. Both sets of legislation allow states to develop policies that are consistent with traditional state practices. As a result, measures that appear to be commonly defined on the federal level may in practice have slight variations across the states. Readers are asked to keep this in mind while perusing the measures defined in the next several sections. The next sections lay out these basic accountability measures currently specified by both acts.

Workforce Investment Act Accountability Provisions

WIA introduced a new set of federal accountability measures that are intended to focus on employment outcomes while setting flexible performance standards.

Table 5.1. WIA Performance Indicators

| | Subprogram | | | |
Indicator	Adults	Dislocated Workers	Youth, Age 14–18	Youth, Age 19–21
Entry into unsubsidized employment	X	X		X
Retention in unsubsidized employment six months after entry into the employment	X	X		X
Earnings received in unsubsidized employment six months after entry into the employment	X	X		X
Attainment of a recognized credential relating to achievement of educational skills	X	X		X
Attainment of basic skills and, as appropriate, work readiness or occupational skills			X	
Attainment of secondary school diplomas and their recognized equivalents			X	
Placement and retention in postsecondary education, advanced training, military service, employment, or qualified apprenticeships			X	
A single customer satisfaction measure for employers	X	X	X	X
A single customer satisfaction indicator for participants	X	X	X	X

Title I Performance Indicators. The purpose of the WIA Title I was to "provide workforce investment activities through statewide and local workforce investment systems, that increase employment, retention, and earnings of participants, and increase occupational skill attainment by participants, and as a result, improve the quality of the workforce, reduce welfare dependency, and enhance the productivity of competitiveness of the Nation." There are a total of seventeen required measures specified in the WIA for adult, dislocated-worker, and youth programs. Two of them are customer satisfaction measures and cross all three areas, while each of the other fifteen is specific to one of the subpopulations. The list presented here itemizes each of the seventeen required measures, presented by population being measured. It should be noted that there is considerable variation among states in operationalizing these indicators. Much depends, of course, on data availability, especially provision of unit record data needed to make the calculations implied by Table 5.1.

Section 136 of the WIA calls for the use of state unemployment insurance (UI) wage records to gather wage and employment data for former participants. Since this outcome measure lags behind program participation by at least a year, the reporting must lag at least a year behind program participation. Further, although use of UI data to track for this purpose is mandated, some states, citing the federal Family Education and Related Privacy Act, have prohibited further use of these data, a stance that inhibits the ability of local programs to test other outcomes.

Each state is required to submit a plan that will propose the expected level of performance for each of the seventeen indicators. States are allowed to develop additional performance measures, but they are not included in any incentive or sanction processes the federal Department of Labor may use. The U.S. secretary of labor and the state's governor must come to agreement on level of performance for the WIA. The plans were to include:

- Baseline performance data and expected level of performance for each of the seventeen measures
- The extent to which the expected level of performance would result in attaining a high level of customer satisfaction
- How expected levels would compare to national averages
- The extent to which such performance levels promote continuous improvement and ensure optimal return on investment of federal funds

As part of the negotiation process, states were allowed to use a variety of "environmental" factors to modify performance level, such as economic conditions (for example, unemployment rate), characteristics of the participants (such as indicators of educational level), services to be provided (including the extent of non-Title I training money available), or other factors (Stevens, 2001).

States would then be evaluated on their performance for sanctions and incentives. Sanctions and incentives were based on the extent to which the state exceeded, met, or fell below negotiated performance levels. If a state negotiated one rate to be 75 percent but only achieved 50 percent, then it would have achieved 66.7 percent of the goal. If, on the other hand, the state reached 75 percent it would achieve 100 percent of the negotiated goal.

The data will be aggregated by the U.S. Department of Education such that each program area will have a score, rather than a score for each of the seventeen measures. As a result, the four program areas (adults, dislocated workers, and youth—both older and younger) and customer satisfaction will have aggregate scores. If a state has unacceptable performance in two consecutive years, a monetary sanction may be imposed. In addition, states may be sanctioned for failure to submit a state performance progress report on time.

Title II Performance Indicators. WIA Title II was developed with its purpose being "to assist adults to become literate and obtain the knowledge and skills necessary for reemployment and self-sufficiency . . . and to become full partners in the educational development of their children." It is the purpose of this title to create a partnership among the federal government, states, and localities to provide voluntarily adult education and literacy services, in order to (1) assist adults in becoming literate and obtaining the knowledge and skills necessary for employment and self-sufficiency, (2) help adults who are parents obtain the educational skills necessary to become full partners in the educational development of their children, and (3) assist adults in completing a secondary school education.

These are the core indicators for WIA Title II:

- Demonstrated improvement in level of reading, writing, speaking the English language, numeracy, problem solving, English language acquisition, and other literacy skills
- Placement in, retention in, or completion of postsecondary education, training, unsubsidized employment, or career advancement
- Receipt of a secondary school diploma or its recognized equivalent

As with Title I, each state may include additional indicators of performance in the plan, as well as allowance for adjustment to the level of performance on each of the core indicators.

Institutional Eligibility Measures. For a college or other entity to offer training under WIA, the training program and provider had to be deemed eligible by the local Workforce Investment Board. Initial eligibility was open to postsecondary institutions eligible for funds from Title IV of the Higher Education Act or the National Apprenticeship Act, or an institution or organization that was "another public or private provider of a program of training services" and approved by the local Workforce Investment Board (WIB) on the basis of criteria specified by the state's governor.

Subsequent eligibility as a training provider was determined by each WIB under the WIA provision that "each Governor of a State shall establish a procedure for use by local boards in the State in determining the eligibility of a provider." Each state is required to collect a number of performance measures:

- The program completion rate for all individuals participating in the applicable program conducted by the provider
- The percentage of all individuals participating in the applicable program who obtain unsubsidized employment, which may also include information specifying the percentage of individuals who obtain unsubsidized employment in an occupation related to the program conducted
- The wages at placement in employment of all individuals participating in the applicable program

In addition, states were to require certain training services information for all program participants:

- The percentage of participants who have completed the applicable program and who are placed in unsubsidized employment

- The retention rate in unsubsidized employment of participants who have completed the applicable program, six months after the first day of the employment
- The wages received by participants who have completed the applicable program, six months after the first day of the employment involved
- Where appropriate, the rate of licensure or certification, attainment of academic degree or equivalent, or attainment of other measures of skills on the part of the graduates of the applicable program
- Information on program costs (such as tuition and fees) for participants in the applicable program

The governor may also require that a provider submit:

- Retention rate in employment and the subsequent wages of all individuals who complete the applicable program
- Where appropriate, the rate of licensure or certification of all individuals who complete the program
- The percentage of individuals who complete the program who attain industry-recognized occupational skills in the subject, occupation, or industry for which training is provided through the program, where applicable

These criteria, as originally devised, served as a significant impediment to many colleges desiring to furnish WIA training. In essence, every program a college made available to WIA participants would need to have all of the data listed here for all of the program participants—not just the WIA participants. The effort this required led many community colleges to question the cost of complying with these mandates, balanced against the funds they were to receive.

Perkins III Accountability Provisions. The purpose of Perkins III is "to develop more fully the academic, vocational, and technical skills of secondary students and postsecondary students who elect to enroll in vocational and technical programs." Core indicators of performance, as written in the law, are:

- Student attainment of challenging state-established academic, and vocational and technical, skill proficiencies
- Student attainment of a secondary school diploma or its recognized equivalent, a proficiency credential in conjunction with a secondary school diploma, or a postsecondary degree or credential
- Placement in, retention in, and completion of postsecondary education or advanced training, placement in military service, or placement or retention in employment
- Student participation in and completion of vocational and technical education programs that lead to nontraditional training and employment

Each state is allowed to add additional indicators, as indicated in section 113(b)(2)(B): "Additional indicators of performance.—An eligible agency, with input from eligible recipients, may identify in the State plan additional indicators of performance for vocational and technical education activities authorized under the title." As a relief to states that may already have assessment measures in place, Section 113 (b)(2)(C) declares: "If a State previously has developed State performance measures that meet the requirements of this section, the State may use such performance measures to measure the progress of vocational and technical education students."

A review of the Perkins III accountability measures indicates that they are less proscriptive than those found in the WIA. However, Section 113 (b)(3)(A)(i) does lend some guidance for establishing a metric for the core indicators just mentioned: "The levels of performance established under this subparagraph shall, at a minimum—(I) be expressed in a percentage or numerical form, so as to be objective, quantifiable, and measurable; and (II) require the State to continually make progress toward improving the performance of vocational and technical education students."

Accountability Assessment Reform. In 2003, a move was undertaken to try to use common measures across job training and employment programs. The Office of Management and Budget developed a list of common measures to be used across five programs primarily affecting six departments: Labor, Education, Health and Human Services, Veterans Affairs, Interior, and Housing and Urban Development (OMB, 2003). The extent to which this initiative will affect reauthorization of either Perkins III or WIA or both is unknown.

Four common measures are under consideration: (1) attainment of a job, (2) attainment of a certificate or degree by program participants, (3) earnings gains, and (4) total program cost per placement in a job. The first three of these measures are consistent with those already in use under WIA. The last one is intended to be an efficiency measure and was not previously collected as part of the WIA. When these measures are also compared to the Carl D. Perkins act reporting structure, the first two have clear parallels, but unlike the WIA, Perkins III does not have an earnings measure.

There are many issues with the workforce training accountability system as it was originally implemented. The accountability assessment reform previously mentioned indicates that there have been attempts to address some of these issues. However, there are other issues that need to be resolved. A report from the General Accounting Office (2001) indicated that colleges and states "need tools to address the burden associated with conflicting program requirements and clarification about the confusion surrounding the allowed use of social security numbers (SSNs) under the FERPA (20 U.S.C. § 1232g; 34 CFR Part 99) and related policy guidance to meet data collection requirements."

First and foremost, accountability measures across all workforce training programs should be consistent. Colleges should not have to furnish varying data for the different programs, often for the same course or aca-demic program.

The underlying tension between developing a system that allows states control over how workforce training services are provided and mandating uniform measures across states will continue to be a difficult issue to deal with. However, since states are measured against themselves for incentive and sanction purposes, it would seem that comparability across states should be of secondary importance. In addition, many states have methods of measuring programmatic efficacy that may not fit the definitions imposed by statute. Therefore, a system that allowed workforce training providers to use existing data would greatly reduce the cost and burden on intuitions.

Finally, if colleges are to fully participate in workforce training pro-grams, the burden of reporting must be manageable. Many community col-leges have a large number of programmatic offerings and students who flow between programs, making comparison between WIA and non-WIA stu-dents difficult to track. Colleges need to be accountable for the programs they are offering, giving potential students a realistic perspective of what to expect. Most colleges have data available to them that they can give to prospective students, and they should be enabled to use those data, rather than federally mandated measures that are onerous to the point of causing colleges to opt out of participating in federally funded programs.

The workforce training system in the United States is not federal but rather a collection of state systems that deal with public and private institu-tions, to deliver training and services to those in need. As such, a one-size-fits-all paradigm does not work. Any accountability system will require that states have the flexibility to use existing data and use measures that are sen-sitive to the issues faced by the particular institutions providing the training.

Implications for Institutional Researchers

The institutional research office is increasingly overwhelmed by federal, state, and local requests for measures designed to assess institutional accountability for federal, state, and local funds. When state and federal funds become scarce, the impact that negative accountability results have on an institution can be significant. It is therefore critical that the local IR office be aware of these accountability measures, and what the institutional data resources must be to adequately respond to those requests. In some cases, there may be opposing demands from state and local accountability requests, and the IR office has to understand the political implications of one set of accountability results versus another set of results—often for the same program.

As the workforce and training legislature is revisited and eventually enacted, the current measures reported on will change. IR offices are in a unique position to extend input and comments on pending legislature and regulations. Although individuals may not have the power to change or modify legislature, by presenting a voice during the process a collective group of individuals may be able to affect the legislation, or regulations that result from the legislation.

The earlier the IR office is aware of the proposed or enacted legislation and resultant regulations, the easier it will be to prepare for the new reporting demands placed on their systems. If the IR office is late in becoming aware of the new reporting standards, there is potential for funding restrictions or possible sanctions against the institution.

References

Carl D. Perkins Vocational and Applied Technology Education Amendments of 1998, Public Law 105–332, 105th Congress, 1998.

European Commission. "Leonardo da Vinci Community Vocational Training Action Programme Second Phase: 2000–2006." Retrieved Sept. 25. 2005, http://europa.eu.int/comm/education/programmes/leonardo/new/leonardo2/guides/en_6.doc. (n.d.)

General Accounting Office. *Workforce Investment Act: Better Guidance Needed to Address Concerns over New Requirements.* Washington, D.C.: General Accounting Office, 2001.

Manning, S., and Lasonen, J. "Finnbase: Enhancing the Attractiveness of Vocational Education. A Knowledge Base on Finnish and European Experience." Retrieved Mar. 1, 2005, http://www.b.shuttle.de/wifo/finn/dk-02-fi.htm. 2005.

OMB Director's Memorandum. "M-02–06, Training and Employment Notice No. 8–02, Implementation of Common Performance Measures for Job Training and Employment Programs." Retrieved Oct. 6, 2004, http://www.whitehouse.gov/omb/budintegration/common.html. 2003.

Stevens, D. W. "21st Century Accountability: Perkins III and WIA." Information Paper 1002. National Dissemination Center for Career and Technical Education, Ohio State University, Columbus, 2001.

Workforce Investment Act of 1998, Public Law 105–220, 105th Congress, 1998.

KENT A. PHILLIPPE *is senior research associate at the American Association of Community Colleges.*

6

Institutions benefit from working directly with employers to adjust their curricula and qualification frameworks to ensure student success in labor markets.

Working with Business and Industry to Enhance Curriculum Development and Student Employability

Sven Junghagen

This chapter is a case study of how one institution worked with internal and external constituents to support student employability. The Graduate School of Business at Copenhagen Business School (CBS), working through curriculum development and a communications plan, has embedded employability both pedagogically and practically into a complex set of interrelated programs of study. The lessons that faculty and staff of CBS have learned may be helpful to other academic departments that seek to appropriately tie their curricula to industry needs. It is not intended as a best practice per se, but rather as "a practice"—a description of implemented and intended activities leading to an overriding goal: establishment of a qualifications framework relying on continuous curriculum development to support student employability.

The very process of creating a qualifications framework has induced a healthy discussion on curriculum development across the college, mainly because it is devoted to the future expected practice for our graduates. In particular, we focus on the Graduate School of Business (GSB), which encompasses the master of science (M.Sc.) and master of arts (M.A.) programs. GSB was initially established as an integrated part of the Faculty of Economics and Business Administration with the aim of strengthening coordination of the development of curricula, pedagogical principles, evaluation policies and marketing of M.Sc. programs in economics, business administration, and related areas. (In Denmark, as in much of Europe, it is traditional for students to take master's courses during their studies rather than stopping at bachelor's level courses; hence the large number of students and master's options at CBS. The differentiation between bachelor's and master's programs, with the master's as a final qualification, is a recent change in Europe owing to the Bologna Declaration.)

There are in all twenty-eight alternatives for M.Sc./M.A. education at GSB in academic year 2004–05. These programs create complexity in terms of academic directions and structures, and for this reason we focus on the general M.Sc. program in economics and business administration here. The program (cand.merc., in Danish) at CBS Graduate School of Business encompasses fifteen lines, or subprograms, within the degree in academic year 2004–05. Each line consists of mandatory core courses in the first year, elective courses in the third semester, and a master's thesis in the fourth semester (EN indicates that all core courses in the line are taught in English).

1. AEF, Applied Economics and Finance (EN)
2. ESG, Economics of International Strategy and Governance (EN)
3. FSM, Finance and Strategic Management (EN)
4. IBS, International Business Studies (EN)
5. IMM, International Marketing and Management (EN)
6. MCM, Marketing Communications Management (EN)
7. MIB, Management of Innovation and Business Development (EN)
8. DCM, Design and Communication Management
9. EMF, Marketing Economics
10. FIR, Finance and Accounting
11. HRM, Human Resource Management
12. IMP, Industrial Marketing and Purchasing
13. MAC, Management, Accounting, and Communication
14. SCM, Supply Chain Management
15. SOL, Strategy, Organization, Management

All fifteen lines of the M.Sc. program in economics and business administration constitute a progression on top of the B.Sc. degree. Students acquire the generalist qualifications at the B.Sc. level on which the M.Sc. program builds, providing a specialist qualification within one of the fifteen options. Structured in this way, the B.Sc. and M.Sc. programs result in generalist and specialist qualifications during a five-year period.

The specialist qualifications are ensured by the various lines in the first year of the study and the final master's thesis in the fourth semester. During the third semester, the students are free to make a choice when taking electives and can opt to broaden their scope into other areas within economics and business administration, or they can strengthen their qualifications within their field of specialization. This progression within the specialization is, in some lines, afforded by line specific progression courses.

Pedagogy at GSB

Even though the details of pedagogy differ among the lines—mainly because of didactic elements in different thematic fields—some commonalities build on the shared pedagogical principles of CBS. To take an example, one can compare the line Human Resource Management (HRM) with Applied Economics and Finance (AEF). In HRM, the conceptual focus is on the human being as learning individual, resulting in a pedagogical approach where the process is more important than the content. In AEF, there are a number of well-defined tools—in, for example, econometrics and finance—that students need to master, resulting in an approach where the content is more important than in HRM. Even though these differences occur, the primary goal for all programs is to enable the students to:

- Take responsibility for and organize their own learning process
- Apply theories analytically to issues and problems faced by companies
- Work methodically with the problems and issues contained in the subjects
- Reflect critically on the foundation and relevance of the theories
- Develop personal and interpersonal competence

These are the central common elements in CBS pedagogy:

- The courses of study build on the concept that contact hours should accelerate the student's learning process, but the most important part of the learning process takes place outside contact hours.
- A mixture of varied, activating teaching methods is applied that take into consideration study level and pedagogic differences. Special emphasis is placed on dialogue, case studies, and project work.
- Information technology is incorporated wherever it can be used to promote learning and effectiveness.
- Examination forms and incentive structures should support the primary pedagogic goals.
- The primary goals as well as the specific academic goals of the individual program determine the priority given to the scope of the subject and its academic content.
- The nuts and bolts are integrated as much as possible into the core subjects. Alternatively, the core subjects define the content of the nuts and bolts and the problem-based cases that the subjects build on.
- Emphasis is placed on giving the students considerable freedom of choice, in the form of optional subjects or lines.

The M.Sc. program is research-based. This does not necessarily imply that a researcher affiliated with CBS should be the one handling all pedagogical contact with students. The learning process is a reflection and representation of a research setting, where it is the student who has the main responsibility for his or her own outcome of this process. Continuous dialogue and critical reflection are the foundation for a learning context where knowledge is created rather than distributed. The next section of this chapter accounts for how these pedagogical principles have been made operational in the M.Sc. (cand.merc.) program at GSB, and how these principles have been interrelated within the concept of future expected practice for graduates.

Toward a Qualifications Framework

Even though CBS is a self-governed independent institution, it has an obligation to enter into a performance contract with the Danish Ministry of Science, Technology, and Innovation. In the performance contract for the period 2000–2003, CBS committed the university to define qualifications frameworks for all study programs at CBS, a process initiated in the beginning of 2003. Thus the process of creating the qualifications framework for the M.Sc. (cand.merc.) program began not long ago (Junghagen and Tofteskov, 2004).

CBS Learning Lab (the unit responsible for pedagogical development at CBS) initiated the process by publishing an inspirational note on the development of qualifications frameworks (Andersen and others, 2003). To aid faculty understanding of qualifications frameworks, a conceptual model for curriculum development was introduced (Figure 6.1).

Figure 6.1. Development Model

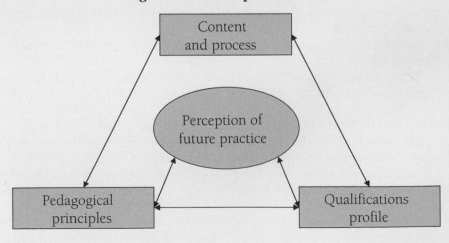

Source: Andersen and others (2003).

The central dimension of this model is the perception of future practice for graduates. This perception is expected to develop over time and is dependent on information gathered by way of ongoing relations with industry through research activities, contacts with alumni, and other industry contacts. This perception then gives rise to a certain qualification profile of graduates needed to live up to the requirements in future practice. Together, these two dimensions constitute competency goals for the study program. To reach competency goals requires the presence of the two other dimensions. The content and process of the program together with the pedagogical principles need to be aligned with the competency goals, so that the program is consistent throughout the process of creating the qualifications framework.

Defining a Perception of Future Practice

To define a perception of a future practice of graduates is quite complex. One can always rely on specific job functions—as we know them today—but this is not enough to guide curriculum development. Close relations with the business community are of crucial importance. This is not to say that business schools should deliver exactly what the business community requests. An important role for a business school is not only to follow trends and development in industry but also to function as an actor taking part in driving and stimulating this development. At the same time, continuous input from industry is essential to define future practice; it is achieved through research partnerships, student projects in industry, advisory boards, external examiners, CBS alumni, and corporate relations at the CBS Career Center. It should be noted that this is not a formal process of identifying job profiles as one would see, for example, in a designing a curriculum (DACUM) approach.[1] Instead, the process described in this chapter has emerged organically, identifying multiple relevant sources of input.

Research partnerships are not directly linked to educational activities or curriculum development, but they do function as an important source of information from the business community. At CBS, there is a natural link to industry in most of the research activities. Corporations enter formal partnership agreements in creating research centers or act as industry partners in individual research projects. This continuous contact helps faculty get an initial sense of direction about future practice.

Student projects in industry are another important *ad hoc* source of information. Since faculty act as advisers for these students, they develop an impression of what will be expected from a future graduate in relation to the individual professor's academic field.

Advisory boards function as a more systematic input. Academic staff have the opportunity to get more objective-oriented input about specific issues identified in other (nonacademic) settings. Advisory boards are not used directly for curriculum development but are able to give valuable input about future practice and what might be lacking in terms of content in a number of programs.

External examiners are used systematically in the Danish system for higher education. They take part in written and oral exams at CBS, and they have a significant influence on student grading. But more important, their role is to monitor the content and process of exams, and to make sure that students taking their exams do have qualifications that are wanted in the business community. These external examiners have a governing body, which is responsible for giving systematic feedback to the Danish institutions.

CBS alumni contribute insightfully to curriculum development, since they have first-hand experience of the study programs along with their experience in business practice. The lines of specialization have their own alumni club, parallel to the overall CBS alumni association. This is an opportunity to have a closer link between specific alumni and a particular program.

The CBS Career Center has an obvious position with its close contact to the business community and the potential career paths of GSB graduates. The close relation between the faculty and the Career Center has helped a lot in defining the qualification frameworks and continuous curriculum development. The CBS Career Center does, of course, emphasize student employability when contributing to the development processes.

Defining Qualifications

The task of defining qualification frameworks is not isolated to CBS or Denmark; there is a movement toward harmonization of higher education in Europe, expressed in the Bologna Declaration, whose purpose is creation of a European area for higher education before 2010 to enable students and graduates to move freely between European education institutions and national labor markets. This necessitates recognition of education units and complete programs within the entire area. To define comparability between programs, the chosen focus is competency goals. The national working group for implementation of the Bologna declaration in Denmark has chosen to focus on three levels of competency goals:

1. *Intellectual competencies,* such as analytical and abstract thinking, a knowledge-seeking approach, communications skills, and the ability to structure one's own learning. These are general competencies that are neither narrow nor directly related to a specific program or discipline.
2. *Professional and academic competencies,* such as specialist competencies within a specific discipline, insight into related disciplines, and cross-disciplinary competencies. These competencies are specifically related to each individual program or discipline.
3. *Practical competencies,* such as practical skills, professional ethics, and responsibility. Competencies of this type are aimed specifically at fulfilling

job functions. For some education programs, these competencies are developed specifically, while for others they are an expected outcome upon completion of the program.

This working group has proposed operational conclusions for M.Sc. programs in Denmark: "An MSc graduate will have competencies that have been acquired via a course of study that has taken place in a research environment. An MSc graduate should be qualified for employment on the labor market on the basis of his or her academic discipline as well as for further research (PhD programs). An MSc graduate should, compared to a Bachelor, have developed his or her academic knowledge and independence so as to be able to apply scientific theory and method on an independent basis within both an academic and professional context" (Danish Ministry of Science, Technology, and Innovation, 2003, pp. 23–24).

In relation to intellectual competencies, the working group stresses the ability to communicate complex issues; formulate and analyze these issues independently, critically, and systematically; and continue one's own competency development and specialization.

Professional and academic competencies are expressed as the ability to evaluate independently the appropriateness of various methods of analysis and complex academic issues. Furthermore, an M.Sc. graduate should be able to demonstrate a specialist understanding in extension of the bachelor's degree, or a broader academic perspective than in the bachelor's degree, or new academic competencies in addition to those gained in the bachelor's degree. The research dimension is expressed through the ability to demonstrate understanding of research work and, on that basis, be active in a research context, and to demonstrate insight into the implications of research (research ethics).

Finally, *practical competencies* are defined as the ability—in addition to bachelor competencies—to make and justify decisions according to academic discipline and if necessary carry out analyses that result in an adequate basis for decision making; and to comprehend development work on the grounds of scholarly, theoretic, or experimental methods.

These competency levels were chosen as a starting point for defining the qualifications framework for the M.Sc. program in economics and business administration. Since the program is built on fifteen specialization lines, the challenge is to define the commonalities as well as the uniqueness within and across each line. In practice, there are many differences between lines, but the task was to identify the common denominator for all specializations. Since they all represent a specific set of qualifications, in terms of practice and academic competency goals, the key to commonalities was found in the intellectual competency goals. To define a common platform for the specializations, Bloom's taxonomy of cognitive dimensions in learning processes (1956) was used as a conceptual touchstone to create a framework for intellectual competency goals for the M.Sc. program:

- Knowledge of terminology: defined as remembering and recalling appropriate and previously learned information
- Comprehension: grasping and understanding the meaning of informational materials
- Application: use of previously learned information in new and concrete situations to solve a problem that has a single or a best answer
- Analysis: breaking down informational materials into their component parts, examining such information to develop divergent conclusions by identifying motives or causes, making inferences, and finding evidence to support generalizations
- Synthesis: applying prior knowledge and skills creatively to produce a new or original whole
- Evaluation: judging the value of material on the basis of personal values and opinions, leading to a result with a given purpose, without right or wrong answers

A graduate with an M.Sc. in economics and business administration can be expected to have qualifications (in relation to the generalist qualifications) corresponding to knowledge, comprehension, application, and analysis. The specialist qualification also involves the higher-order synthesis and evaluation levels, with the implication that a graduate has the ability, when confronted with a novel problem or issue in practice, to solve it by means of new and previously unknown problem solutions. This is the basis of synthesis and evaluation, to be able to combine existing knowledge creatively and discover new solutions of unknown problems in this combination of existing solutions.

The question then turns to how these qualifications can be embedded within a program of study. For a student to solve existing problems with known solutions requires little reflection and is actually quite simple. The student needs only to understand the problem and know his or her toolbox. What moves one up the scale to higher-order thinking tasks is reflective ability, understanding the meta-theoretical foundations of theory, which in turn builds a foundation of problem solutions (Figure 6.2).

There are four basic levels common to all specializations:

1. Issues in economics and business administration refer to the perceived future practice for our students. Each of the fifteen lines has its own set of issues, leading to differences in defining professional, academic, and practical competencies.

2. Models and tools are used to solve these issues, which in turn build on various theoretical foundations. These models and tools are basically the best solutions to problems as we know them today.

3. Theory is the foundation for models and tools. This does not necessarily mean theory in just economics and business administration but also in the behavioral sciences, including sociology and psychology. Tools and

Figure 6.2. Levels of Understanding

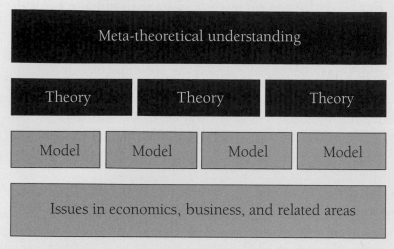

models build on different theoretical starting points, and an M.Sc. graduate should be able to show an understanding of these differences.

4. Meta-theoretical understanding is needed for deeper understanding of theory. There are a number of relationships and differences within and between paradigms and perspectives. To understand theory, and to have the ability to actively work with theory, this understanding is crucial.

All M.Sc. graduates are expected to have a solid and broad understanding of the various issues and problems in economics and business administration, and the tools and methods needed to solve these problems. The theoretical understanding is also expected to be broad. Furthermore, an M.Sc. graduate is expected to have a meta-theoretical understanding, helping to comprehend theoretical paradigms describing a given issue from a number of perspectives. This ability helps the student actively reflect on issues and make him or her able to synthesize at the model level to work creatively with issues in practice.

Content and Pedagogical Principles

Having defined the expected future practice and a qualification profile to match this practice, it is then necessary to define the study content and specific pedagogical approaches. Broadly, a study program can be constructed from two perspectives: focusing on content at one extreme, and focusing on the learning process at the other. At GSB, content is of course crucially important, but the M.Sc. program puts most of its focus on the learning process, which is reflected in the pedagogical principles of CBS, as stated earlier.

Development of content and pedagogy go hand in hand, since a qualification has been defined not just as knowing something in particular but dealing with problems and issues in a certain way. Every course in a line supports development of the qualification profile of graduates. If this principle is taken to its limit, every single lecture should be defined as supporting the aim of the course, which is to support the overall profile. To view the content and progression as a means-and-ends hierarchy is not a self-fulfilling purpose but serves more as a guideline for reflection on curriculum development. The intellectual competency goals mentioned earlier are achieved mostly on the basis of the learning process, while the practical and academic goals are reflected in the line-specific content and didactic models.

A Systematic Follow-up on Activities

As has been described, the business community contributes valuable input to definition of qualification frameworks. As with all product development and marketing processes, though, it is also important to maintain these input mechanisms in order to continuously develop the study programs. In addition to qualitative input through the channels previously described, GSB has also conducted a survey in the business community, with the aim of exploring dimensions of the qualification framework and the importance of these dimensions. This study takes a multivariate approach, based on a conceptual model shown in Figure 6.3.

All dimensions in Figure 6.3 are latent variables, measured by means of a number of items in the questionnaire. The dimensions were tested through explorative factor analyses, and relations were estimated with path analysis and partial least squares regression. CBS's overall reputation functions as the dependent variable, and it was possible to define what influence each independent factor has, directly as well as indirectly, on reputation (Martensen and Grønholdt, 2005). It was then possible to define how CBS and GSB perform in each dimension and what importance these dimension have on reputation, which led to a reputation score card supporting decisions for future action. The reputation scorecard has functioned as an important tool, since GSB does not want to allocate resources to improve a field lacking a significant effect on its reputation in industry.

The Role of Integrated Communications

The process that has been described here, which aimed to define a qualification framework, has now led to a need to communicate the findings, externally as well as internally. Although the document accounting for the framework consists of approximately sixty pages, external and internal communication has to be more condensed and precise. In the process, a discussion was initiated with the CBS communications department, the in-house unit for corporate communication.

Figure 6.3. Conceptual Model for CBS M.Sc. Reputation

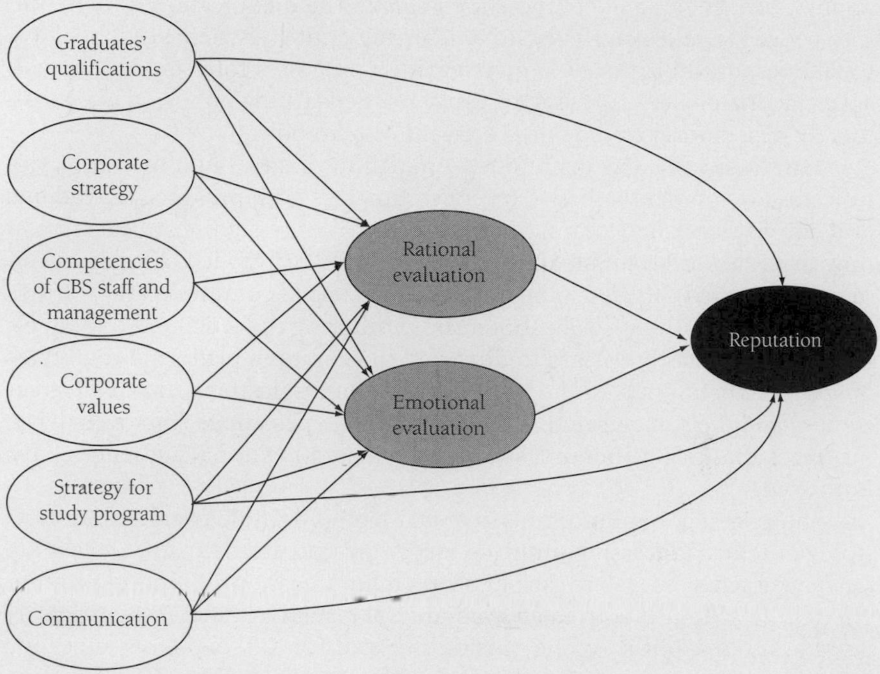

Source: Martensen and Grønholdt (2005).

The first issue addressed was the one related to student recruitment. Communication with prospective students has traditionally been in the form of catalogue material that described each of the study programs in detail, though technically. The continuous contact between CBS Communications and stakeholders provided valuable input for a new paradigm for message strategies for GSB. A prospective student is of course interested in the curriculum and the kind of pedagogy applied, but first and foremost the student is interested in the prospective outcome of the program, that is, whether his or her participation leads to employment. Thus we focused more on the actual qualification framework for the programs while attempting to find the common denominators for them. Since the programs represent quite different practical competency goals, the commonalities are instead defined using intellectual competencies and an overall pedagogical approach. This process resulted in publicity materials that reflected these commonalities.

There are two main arguments in the publicity campaign in 2004. The main message is "CBS Graduate School of Business—Where knowledge is created, not only distributed," supported by a quote: "Not only do you learn to solve well-known problems. You discover how new problems are solved with new problem-solutions." The two arguments have their origin in the applied pedagogies and competency goals in the qualification framework. The pedagogy relies on the creative learning context, where students have to take responsibility for their own learning process. Professors are there to act as facilitators and catalysts to stimulate the learning process, rather than merely distributing a predefined content of textbooks.

On the surface, this might not seem extraordinary, but it was still a significant development in how CBS communicates with prospective students and employers. CBS Communications contributed significant insight on how to extract the commonalities that have been mentioned here, the result of which turned out also to be helpful for internal communication. It has been stated that the specializations show differing didactic methodologies. Historically, it has been hard to illustrate the common platform for all lines of specialization, but with the help of CBS Communications and CBS Career Center, and their understanding of the kind of expectations employers have, messages that GSB communicates to internal and external audiences have improved.

Integrated communications is about using multiple channels, in multiple contexts, addressing multiple target groups. In the main, to develop curricular activities is to engage in deep communication with multiple audiences. The school can, from an academic perspective, have extraordinarily good programs, but if no one outside the walls of the school perceives the product as advantageous, it makes little difference. There are, however, several reasons for a mismatch between expectations and what is delivered. The immediate conclusion is often that something is wrong with the delivery system, but this is not necessarily true. It may be a communication problem, where the challenge is to visualize the qualifications of graduates from the school and convince industry that it can benefit from these qualifications. To support student employability, one needs to communicate. It is not just about getting input from corporate contacts on how to improve programs; it also works the other way around, by creating an understanding within industry of the benefits of qualification profiles.

Conclusion

This chapter suggests some ways in which employability can be embedded and contacts with employers enhanced. Here are perceived positive outcomes of this process at GSB:

- Fundamental tasks are not separate. Research, education, and collaboration with industry should not be treated as asynchronous individual tasks. There are so many synergies among the tasks that they should co-evolve over time.
- Corporate contacts for curriculum development should not be in one direction. Since the task for a business school is not just to follow trends in

industry but to be a driving force of this development, a two-way dialogue with the business community is crucial.

• Communication is not merely a supporting activity. In the value chain, communication is more than information; it is ongoing interaction between parties. How you choose to communicate with the external environment should be reflected in actions and will also affect internal communication.

• Focus on qualifications, not content. It is not likely that a career-oriented prospective student or a prospective employer is particularly interested in the course content of a study program. Instead, they all tend to focus more on the resulting qualifications created during the program. Curriculum development should therefore aim for qualifications and outcomes that are not self-fulfilling but that make a difference in a future practice for the graduate.

Note

1. DACUM is an acronym for *developing a curriculum*. It is a one-or-two-day storyboarding process that yields a picture of what the worker does in terms of duties, tasks, knowledge, skills, and traits, and in some cases the tools the worker uses. The information is presented in graphic chart form and can include critical and frequently performed tasks as well as the training needs of workers. See, for example, http://www.dacum.org/.

References

Andersen, I., Baldur-Felskov, T., Bramming, P., Lillebro, L., and Tofteskov, J. "Kompetenceprofiler, kvalifikationsprofiler og en studieudviklingsmodel—Et inspirationsnotat." CBS Learning Lab. Retrieved Sept. 21, 2005, http://www.ll.cbs.dk/Nyheder.asp?ID=7. 2003.

Bloom, B. (ed.). *Taxonomy of Educational Objectives: The Classification of Educational Goals. Handbook I, Cognitive Domain.* New York: Longmans Green, 1956.

Danish Ministry of Science, Technology, and Innovation. "Towards a Danish Qualifications Framework for Higher Education." Retrieved Sept. 21, 2005, http://www.vtu.dk/fsk/div/bologna/DanishQFReport.pdf. 2003.

Junghagen, S., and Tofteskov, J. (eds.). *Qualifications Framework for MSc in Economics and Business Administration (cand.merc.).* Copenhagen, Denmark: CBS Graduate School of Business, 2004.

Martensen, A., and Grønholdt, L. "Customer Survey in the Business Community." Copenhagen, Denmark: CBS Graduate School of Business, 2004.

SVEN JUNGHAGEN is director and associate professor at the Copenhagen Business School Graduate School, Copenhagen, Denmark.

7

Disadvantaged adult students need special support and clear pathways to economic self-sufficiency. Programs that support them require clear data and information about their success to move forward.

Engaging Institutions in Workforce Development: Career Pathways for Disadvantaged Adults

Julian L. Alssid, David Gruber, Davis Jenkins, Christopher Mazzeo, Brandon Roberts, Regina Stanback-Stroud

The emergence of the global economy has intensified effort by governments to increase the education level of their workforces. Traditionally, education has been one way out of poverty for the unemployed and working poor; today, it is almost the only way. To support a family, move from a low-paying job into a long-term career, and become truly self-sufficient, economically disadvantaged citizens need to be prepared for the new economy, and this means acquiring the education and skills to succeed in a high-wage job.

No matter the nation or part of the world, it is clear that all sectors of higher education must engage in a process of developing large-scale, flexible, and open systems that can offer the education and training required for high-wage, high-demand jobs to all who require them: welfare recipients, unemployed and underemployed workers, at-risk youth, and anyone else with few skills or little education who wants to better his or her job

Note: This chapter is based on the authors' previous publication, Alssid, J. L., Gruber, D., Jenkins, D., Mazzeo, C., Roberts, B., and Stanback-Stroud, R., *Building a Career Pathways System: Promising Practices in Community College-Centered Workforce Development.* Brooklyn, N.Y.: Workforce Strategy Center, 2002. The research was funded by the James Irvine Foundation, the Ford Foundation, the William and Flora Hewlett Foundation, and the Annie E. Casey Foundation.

prospects. Although the more than eleven hundred U.S. community colleges are the most logical—and for all practical purposes the only—foundation for this kind of broad-based workforce development system, it is clear that all sectors of higher education must be engaged in workforce development. Many four-year colleges and universities, like community colleges, combine accessibility to the community, low tuition, a range of education and training offerings, and a continuing funding base. Although many of the examples offered here originate from work in community colleges, there are obvious and important lessons to be gained from that experience to inform other levels of postsecondary education.

Whatever the level, it is clear that bridges to high-wage, high-demand employment for undereducated workers require partnerships. These partnerships include employers, institutions, and students, each of whom is influenced by a labor market increasingly driven by skills and credentials and not necessarily by attainment of a higher degree. Institutions may wish to position themselves as the focal point of regional partnerships that bring together all the key actors in the workforce development system: workforce agencies, community-based organizations, social service agencies, and employers. Working together, these partners can create new "career pathways" that meet the needs of both employers and workers. This chapter highlights research undertaken by the Workforce Strategy Center that documents efforts by colleges and states to create career pathways (Alssid and others, 2002). The research focused on four states—North Carolina, Washington, Florida, and California—and researched best practices at nineteen community colleges and their partner community organizations, workforce investment boards (WIBs), and state and local welfare agencies.

Description of a Career Pathway

The State of New York has invested more than $1 billion in biotechnology infrastructure in the Greater Capital Region over the last eight years in the form of academic laboratory and business incubator construction and new higher-level university curriculum development. The result has been tremendous growth in research and development activities in the region that are seeding the economy with start-up companies, aiding growth in existing companies, and drawing regional transplants of larger companies. At the same time, technological change is occurring at such a rapid pace that regional companies are facing the need to upgrade their workers' skills to stay competitive. This tremendous growth and technological evolution has prompted workforce development policy makers to develop innovated solutions to feed the biotechnology industry with the workers required for continuing its momentum in our region.

The Greater Capital Region Biotechnology Career Pathways Initiative (CPI) is a formed collaboration involving four local WIBs, three local community colleges, and the New York State Department of Labor. Workforce

Strategy Center and New York Association of Training and Employment Professionals are contracted by the New York State Department of Labor to provide technical assistance to the collaboration. Major employers in the capital region are committed as partners to the development of this initiative.

CPI is a collaborative effort to engage biotech companies in career ladder programs that recruit and train unemployed or dislocated workers, particularly from the manufacturing sector, to work in high-demand, high-wage biotech jobs. To redesign the workforce system's operational systems around biotechnology opportunities, CPI realigns the policies and practice of the four WIBs to be more responsive to company needs. Through the collaboration, CPI incorporates customized and on-the-job training targeted to employer needs, builds new partnerships between the WIBs and local colleges, and employs a funding model that creates strong support for these innovative arrangements without excessively taxing WIA resources. To date, new accelerated curricula for laboratory technicians, animal handlers, and biotech manufacturing workers have been developed.

Building and Supporting Career Pathways

Although there are many career pathway models, the most compelling builds a bridge for disadvantaged adults to economic self-sufficiency. This vision of the pathway is essentially just another version of what many middle-class Americans take for granted: a way to identify a promising field and build the necessary competencies to be prepared for a well-paying, long-term career. To move from poverty and poor education to a promising career, the best route is a path that ensures the participant is prepared for the labor market. To successfully advance individuals, a pathway should include:

- An introduction to career opportunities in a region's high-wage, high-demand employment sectors
- The basic skills needed to succeed in postsecondary education and training
- A transition to entry-level skills training
- Internships and employment
- Continuing upgrade training
- Social supports throughout as necessary

Partnerships. Currently, career pathways are by-and-large separate and limited programs, despite their successes. To build a system that is larger and more comprehensive in scope, participants at all three levels—community college, local or regional partner, state government—must become involved. Where the state makes the resources available and local entities work with the community colleges, career pathways constitute a real and powerful opportunity to move economically disadvantaged individuals into well-paying careers.

The community college is typically the center of the career pathway model, but other entities are crucial to its success. In partnership, community-based organizations (CBOs), adult basic education (ABE) providers, and workforce and social service agencies complement and extend pathways; CBOs and social service agencies can recruit individuals isolated from post-secondary education and career opportunities, as well as offer needed social support services during their tenure in the program. Workforce agencies can direct resources toward community colleges to lend financial and operational support in a city or region. ABE providers can offer preparatory services and create a bridge to community college programs. Local employers can help define needed worker skills and offer internships and work sites to deliver upgrade training to workers at all skill levels.

States also have much to say about career pathways. As the primary authority for education, workforce training, and economic development initiatives, states have the potential to encourage and support career pathways. Governors and education and workforce officials can adopt career pathways as the model for training and education for the state workforce development system. States can also encourage pathway development within individual colleges and stimulate strategic partnerships in the surrounding community. Ultimately, the state can commit resources from welfare, workforce, economic development, and community college systems to career pathways. It is worth noting that the federal government plays a similarly important role by furnishing an array of funding that can be used to support this strategy.

Benefits to Institutions. Implementing career pathways can help fulfill the most fundamental mission of the community college: to be an institution that serves all parts of the community. By creating a bridge out of poverty and into well-paying jobs, the school serves low-income, poorly educated constituents in a way that can make a real difference in their lives over the long run. To build career pathways, colleges need to reconcile their many and sometimes conflicting missions and goals by creating new bridges and transitions for students, bringing together traditionally separate faculty (academics), divisions, and resources. By doing so, they allow students in the career pathway to become fully prepared for the workforce.

What benefits accrue to colleges? For college administrators, a career pathways model can serve to:

• Improve student recruitment and increase enrollment, both by offering a new program directly aimed at affording good employment and by raising the profile of the college in the community.
• Improve student retention and success. Career pathways offer a bridge between the large number of students (many of them economically disadvantaged) enrolled in remedial programs and the higher-level, credit-bearing courses that lead to certification, an academic degree, and career employment.

• Raise the stature of the institution, because the college becomes the natural place for business, government, and community leaders to come together to increase the economic viability of the community or region.

• Permit access to new funding by expanding the college's ability to attract students and by building new relationships with employers and funding sources in the broader community and at the state level.

• Improve the quality of education by connecting programs and faculty from workforce, academic, and remedial divisions. The pathway approach can promote learning communities that bring together academic and vocational educators; offer new models for teaching; and help attract and retain talented, energetic, and dedicated faculty members.

Internal Barriers. Community colleges face several barriers in implementing career pathways for disadvantaged students. Overall, community colleges that successfully reconcile their various missions to expand educational and career opportunities for disadvantaged students often do so in spite of prevailing public policies and institutional traditions.

The single largest barrier to creating a successful career pathway is reconciling the community college's various distinct missions, departments, and programs. Divisions are sometimes fueled by the perception that integration with other departments will compromise or water down the department's core mission. It is hard to overstate the effects of separate and distinct missions on college structure; course offerings; and faculty hiring, teaching, and career paths. For example, it is typical for contract (and sometimes vocational) education divisions to work closely with industry in understanding and responding to labor market needs. Frequently, however, the connections to local employers do not extend beyond the department, limiting the opportunity to shape college career programs with both academic and vocational offerings. Long-standing, entrenched divisions between departments are difficult to overcome, particularly for an institution struggling to maintain student enrollment and college operations in a time of considerable budget pressure.

In general, community colleges seldom view noncredit remedial and vocational coursework as a feeder for degree programs, even though many students in adult literacy programs and vocational training programs might well be interested in pursuing this route. The result of this separation is that students can be forced to choose between a track that leads to a degree and one that leads to employment.

Furthermore, without defined career pathways, students are given little information on their educational options in other departments and programs and face bureaucratic barriers to advancement. Disadvantaged students are the least likely to be able to negotiate an educational system that fails to offer clear guidance and support to help them advance.

Here are some of the ways in which conflicting missions inside an institution manifest themselves:

• Vocational training programs often do not carry credit toward a degree, even when their content is similar to that of courses taken for a degree. This issue is even more difficult to remedy where vocational programs for adults are offered by local school districts.

• "Workplace literacy" programs designed to improve the literacy skills of incumbent workers are not offered through the academic divisions of the college, and they do not typically encourage students to pursue a degree with the college.

• Academic faculty members see their role as providing the first two years of general education toward a bachelor's degree, not preparing students for employment. This occurs even though most community college students are employed at least part-time and want both a better job and a college degree.

• Programs that offer an applied or contextual approach to teaching are generally most effective at preparing students for employment in technical fields, but four-year institutions are often reluctant to accept transfer credit for such courses, even if a statewide articulation agreement is in place to facilitate the transfer.

Lack of Resources. A pathway model is more expensive than traditional remedial programming, requiring additional resources for curriculum development, lab facilities, employer and student outreach, and faculty development. Funding for all these objectives is scarce and frequently restricted by regulations and guidelines that can limit the far-reaching changes called for by career pathways.

Because most community college budgets are tied up in salaries for instruction, administrators have limited discretionary money and rely on grant funding to develop new programs or explore new ways of teaching. Once funding from a grant ends, the school may find it difficult to sustain the resulting program. For their part, faculty members are pressed by a high teaching load and generally have little time to develop new programs without extra support. Paying for the discrete parts of a pathway can be difficult as well, especially for the highly individual and contextualized instruction that research shows is effective with academically unprepared adults. Policy makers may disdain funding remedial programs because they think it means "paying twice" for what high schools should have taught students. A study by the Education Commission of the States found that in Georgia, Illinois, and several other states, college remedial programs receive less funding than college-credit courses. It also found at least ten states that either make available no funding for adult basic education (ABE) at community colleges or fund it at a level below that of college-credit programs. Colleges that make serving disadvantaged students a priority have to scramble unceasingly to piece together funding from whatever sources they can find. Such funding is usually of limited duration. Unlike lecture-based academic classes, technical training requires extra equipment, lab time, and relatively small class size, all of which are expenses for which the school receives no extra compensation.

Disadvantaged students also tend to need more support than other students, and this attention is expensive as well. When community colleges do receive direct funding for student support services, it is allocated on a full-time equivalent (FTE) enrollment basis. However, three part-time students may require three times as many support services as one full-time student, so a college with many part-time students struggles to offer adequate support. With insufficient funding, staff members often have a high caseload, making it particularly difficult to serve disadvantaged students with greater needs.

Unfortunately, it will be difficult to change these dynamics. In general, working poor adults lack a strong political voice. Unlike the case with public schools, the role of the community college is often not well understood or appreciated by the public. Unlike public four-year institutions, community colleges tend to lack strong political influence with policy makers. For example, in 2000 voters in Arizona passed Proposition 301, which channeled almost $500 million a year to improving education to enhance the state's economic competitiveness. Even though they helped to draft the legislation, community colleges receive only 3 percent of these funds. The lion's share goes to the K-12 system (85 percent) and the state universities (12 percent). This, until very recently, was a scenario familiar to UK readers, where the further education sector has consistently been underfunded and underappreciated—a situation partially ameliorated by recent government funding decisions and initiatives, such as foundation degrees.

Lack of Incentive to Serve the Disadvantaged. For several reasons, community colleges may place less emphasis on serving disadvantaged students than on other priorities. For example, college-entry proficiency examinations in states such as Texas and North Carolina are required for all students who would be eligible to gain college credit. The need to ensure that educationally disadvantaged applicants are prepared to pass these exams may be a disincentive for colleges to reach out to these students.

The relatively high cost of serving this population, as has been outlined, is another disincentive, especially for a school facing budget cuts in these lean times. Further exacerbating the issue is the question of financial aid. Most community college students work at least part-time in addition to attending school and caring for a family. Even when working, adult students barely make enough to sustain themselves or their families; they often do not qualify for federal or state financial aid, which tends to be designed for full-time students. Furthermore, few states offer financial aid for students in noncredit programs (although in some states adult basic skills and other noncredit programs are offered free of charge).

Power and prestige in many community colleges is concentrated in the academic faculty, who tend to see their role as teaching college-level subject matter and as such are sometimes resentful of having to deal with students who are not prepared for college. To be fair, the problem does not lie solely within the community college itself. Without clear state policy and guidance, a focus on transfer to a baccalaureate program remains the primary measure of success in college, giving little incentive to develop other capacities.

At the same time, circumstances have required colleges to address the gap between remedial and college-level courses. It is not uncommon for community college English and mathematics faculty to spend a majority of their time teaching developmental classes to prepare students for the school's academic coursework. A National Science Foundation–funded study of community college occupational programs in science and technology fields found that the most common problem facing these programs is inadequate academic preparation of entering students (Burton and Celebuski, 1995). Now, nearly a decade later, it is more than likely that inadequate preparation continues to plague the efforts of community college educators to produce job-ready graduates.

Promising Practices

Research found that six basic steps are necessary to create career pathways (Alssid and others, 2002): (1) community outreach to economically and educationally disadvantaged adults; (2) basic skills coursework at community-based organizations that serve as "branch campuses" of the local community college; (3) entry-level training in a career or technical area; (4) internship placement; (5) entry-level employment in the field of preparation; and (6) upgrade training, postemployment. Not every participant will necessarily take advantage of each component of a pathway like this. One student may be able to go directly to the entry-level training without any basic skills coursework, for example, while another may never use the upgrade training. By presenting a comprehensive set of training and education, with clear progression built in, the system ensures that all students are prepared for their new career, no matter on what level they enter the pathway.

Developing career pathways requires changing how a community college structures and delivers education and career training to the community as a whole and to economically disadvantaged adults in particular. There is considerable work ahead for any college wishing to participate in the career pathways model. Our research shows that six practices are promising for institutions in pursuit of this model:

1. Creating bridge programs between developmental and credit-bearing programs
2. Developing internal career pathways leading to certification and college degrees
3. Expanding support services
4. Integrating academic and vocational education

5. Integrating administrative structures
6. Using college resources effectively

First, creating connections between remedial and credit-bearing courses, and in a larger sense between remedial programs and career pathways, is a critical policy. Community colleges need to develop formal bridge programs that make remedial education more relevant to adults seeking career training and economic advancement, and that also constitute a direct transition to credit-bearing courses and career training. Relevance can be achieved by incorporating materials from a specific field into courses such as remedial English, reading, and mathematics. This enables academically unprepared students to participate in career training as they enroll in basic education. Programs that promote contextualized learning make heavy use of projects, laboratories, simulations, and other experiences that enable students to learn by doing.

Second, although students in career pathway programs tend to have as their most immediate priority a decent-paying job, in the long run they need the option of pursuing a college degree, which in most fields is necessary to advance beyond a certain level in a career. A growing number of colleges offer credit for training that leads to industry or professional certifications in fields such as information technology. Students are much more likely to opt for classes that have an established connection between associate degree and bachelor's degree programs. For example, Arizona State University (ASU) and the Maricopa Community College system have established Bridges to Biomedical Careers, which prepares and motivates minority students to progress from an associate to a bachelor's biomedical degree. The program offers students an intensive five-week summer session. Those who complete the summer program receive a stipend and upper-division credit toward a bachelor's degree. They also receive academic support throughout the year and can continue to participate in independent study and research with the ASU faculty.

Portland Community College (Oregon), in partnership with Mount Hood Community College and the local Workforce Industry Board, have created a Regional Workforce Training Team to hold short-term training (three to six months) for dislocated workers with limited English proficiency and low basic skills. Existing curricula at the schools have been reorganized into shorter modules in four fields, which allows students to earn a preliminary certificate and enter a job. Because these short-term modules are part of existing college programs, students are eligible for both federal financial aid and WIA funding.

Third, there are several ways to successfully integrate faculty. A school can integrate the contract staff and faculty members in other departments to create a program and instruction that are responsive to industry. Some colleges create an opportunity for interdisciplinary development of career pathways through a joint committee, formal interdepartmental agreement, or stipend or "buy-out" of time for participating faculty. For some schools, this can even be an explicit strategy for retaining talented faculty members by affording interesting, creative opportunities to expand their professional experience.

Fourth, low-income community college students need support services to successfully balance family, financial, and life issues along with study (Matus-Grossman and Gooden, 2002). Ideally, the various services (assessment, financial aid, counseling, referrals) should be coordinated to extend the full range of support that many students need and to assist struggling students before they drop out. Partnership with community-based organizations, discussed in greater detail in the next chapter, can also furnish additional services that community colleges are generally not well equipped to provide, such as child care, drug treatment, health care, family counseling, and transportation. Partnership also means giving colleges a fruitful recruiting ground for career pathway programs.

Fifth, integration of administrative departments facilitates operation. Colleges that bring together traditionally separate departments under a single administrator gain a significant advantage in their effort to integrate learning, access new resources, and develop career pathways (Alssid and others, 2002). At Las Positas Community College in Livermore, California, each academic dean is responsible for both academic and vocational programs. Occupational programs and faculty in the college enjoy status equal to their academic counterparts, and academic faculty members help design and deliver occupational programs. Academic services and student services also operate under the same administrative unit, allowing student services counselors to better work with faculty members to address student needs.

Sixth, community college instructional funds are the core resource for career pathways. Several states fund noncredit programs and programs for students whose basic skills fall below what is generally required of college credit courses. Typically based on FTE enrollments, this funding is an opportunity to create programs that bridge to college-level programs. California, for example, makes available state resources to support both credit and noncredit basic skills instruction. Colleges in California can combine traditional FTEs and separate basic skills and noncredit instructional resources to create a pathway model. In some instances, the Carl D. Perkins Vocational and Applied Technology Education Act (Perkins III) has been used to develop career pathway programs and support faculty development to make them effective. Although Perkins III is typically thought of as a source of funding for equipment, the program's guidelines encourage efforts to increase student access, retention, and success in vocational programs that lead students to a position in the workforce.

Building Strategic Partnerships in the Community and the Region. Clearly, even if they have the necessary vision, individual community colleges often lack the resources and capacity to implement pathways successfully without assistance. On a large scale, effective career pathways require strategic partnership with the key local and regional institutions: employers, workforce agencies, social service agencies, adult education providers, and community-based organizations. By working together, local and regional institutions can build on each organization's strengths to attain a sum greater than its parts. Businesses routinely use similar alliances, forming a partnership with another firm to acquire new competencies. Effective community and regional career pathways are a benefit to both the system itself and to the participating institutions (Alssid and others, 2002).

By joining a career pathway, participating institutions can expand their funding base, broaden their reach and scope, and give students and clients new opportunities. Employers can count on better-prepared workers, for example, and social service agencies can help their clients move out of poverty. The opportunities go beyond each community. Citywide or regional partnerships have even more potential for success, given their reach and ability to attract and leverage stable, long-term funding.

Partnerships with the Workforce and Social Service Systems. The workforce and social service system includes One-Stop Centers, welfare agencies, and organizations that provide training and support services. These government and nonprofit agencies are the main contact point with a community's poorest residents and therefore a source of potential students, many of whom would never otherwise step onto a college campus. Workforce and social service agencies also handle some of the support services needed to help individuals succeed in a college setting, such as counseling, day care, transportation, employability preparation, and substance abuse counseling. For any collaboration, outside resources and encouragement—such as a state mandate, new public or private funding, or a regional vision held by influential leaders—is quite useful in encouraging a career pathways framework.

Workforce agencies are also an important source of funding, particularly in large cities. Los Angeles and New York City both receive more than $70 million in WIA funding, resources that can be used to support services including counseling and outreach, training, and employer subsidies. WIA individual training vouchers, which can vary from $2,000 per person to $5,000 or more, can be spent on training at a community college.

Temporary Assistance for Needy Families (TANF) funding is also a significant (although declining) source of funding. Nevertheless, states such as Washington and North Carolina have used some of this funding to support a statewide career pathway initiative, and among cities Denver and San Francisco have designated a portion of TANF funding to support career progression.

Partnership with Community-Based Organizations. Community colleges and community-based organizations are ideally situated to work together. CBOs, as the institutions closest to the neighborhood, are both accessible and credible to adults who are isolated from educational institutions and training programs. In many communities, CBOs have evolved to amount to a self-contained workforce and social service system, offering a full spectrum of services: counseling, case management, social support, rehabilitative services, and frequently education and training. According to a study by the National Congress for Community Economic Development (NCCED, 2002), 30 percent of community development corporations offer employment and training programs, and nearly half offer some kind of education and training programs. However, CBOs are often limited by lack of resources and few connections to employers, and they are generally unable to offer the quality and depth of education and skills training clients need to attain self-sufficiency.

Community colleges have the resources and capacity to offer a full spectrum of education and skills training. Yet they often have difficulty effectively serving individuals who need additional support to succeed in a challenging and unfamiliar environment, a reality underlined by a high dropout rate in many institutions. Moreover, as a recent Manpower Demonstration Research Corporation study suggests, many low-income individuals may not even reach community college through lack of awareness of the available services that help ensure success in postsecondary education.

Community college-CBO partnerships link college educational resources with CBO accessibility and support services. Basic skills and entry-level instruction offered to clients at the CBO can become the first step of an integrated career pathway that leads to more advanced training and courses offered on the college campus. Some colleges have made the step easier by establishing a satellite branch campus, teaching credit-bearing courses at the community group's site.

Partnership of this kind offers all parties clear advantages. The college obtains a recruitment source for students and can use the additional resources generated by new enrollment to subsidize instruction at the CBO site. The CBO focuses on areas of strength, such as case management and social support, and expands the quality and range of its educational offerings. CBO clients are able to start on a postsecondary career pathway in an accessible and nonintimidating setting.

Partnerships with Adult Basic Education Providers. The adult basic education (ABE) system, whether operated by a community college, the local school district, or a community-based organization, is a primary vehicle for reaching low-wage, low-skill adults. Typically, they offer reading and basic mathematics, but few focus on career progression and transition to postsecondary education and training as a primary goal. Even ABE programs operated by community colleges frequently lack any formal connection to credit-bearing postsecondary training that leads to higher-skill, higher-wage jobs.

Nevertheless, ABE is potentially an ideal foundation for the first phase of a career pathway, imparting basic education skills to a broad population who are otherwise disconnected from the postsecondary system. An ABE program can be a site for bridge programs that offer career orientation, work readiness, and contextualized basic skills, with a direct transition to a partner community college. Like CBOs, ABE programs are an untapped institutional resource that can play a significant role in developing career pathways throughout the country.

Partnerships with Employers. Employers obviously are a valuable partner for the community college in developing a career pathway. In addition to offering job and internship placement, local businesses can define worker skills and competencies that are in demand, as well as help pathway partners discern labor market demand. Employer work sites also offer an additional venue for the college to deliver upgrade training to workers at all skill levels. However, many community colleges have limited connections to job opportunities for students. A school may have an "industry advisory board" that offers excellent business contacts for fundraising, curriculum development, and academic standards. Such a board, though, usually has only superficial involvement with student placement. When there is a connection to employers, it tends to be isolated from the rest of the institution. For example, contract training departments, which are hired by local firms to teach specific skills to their workforce, are typically self-supporting and independent of college-credit divisions. They generally do not work with full-time faculty, relying on adjunct instructors with industry experience.

State and local agencies have resources at their disposal that can promote incentives for employers to participate in career pathway programs. WIA-customized job training money and state economic development funding can be spent for upgrade training. For example, California's Employment Training Panel (ETP) sets aside $50 million for training for incumbent workers. Typically, the money is employed in limited programs rather than as a component of career pathways, but there is clear potential to combine economic development funding with workforce dollars and other resources.

State Involvement. Higher education institutions do not function in isolation, and they cannot undertake career pathways without considerable involvement by state government. Institutions must engage state policy makers to think and act differently. Research demonstrates, for example, that states should use workforce and human resource programs to promote labor market advancement of low-wage workers in place of work-first policies (Alssid and others, 2002). States should also encourage incentives and flexibility for educational and social service institutions to work together on career pathways. Unfortunately, in most states community college system policies and practices act as a significant obstacle to implementing the pathways vision. Four specific issues emerged over the course of the research:

1. *Limited resources for career programs and training.* A state often allocates core FTE and other supplemental dollars in a way that actually discourages colleges from engaging in career pathways. Career pathways, at least in the short run, are relatively expensive to create and sustain, yet in

many states no FTE funding goes to noncredit vocational and continuing education courses, and in others such courses receive FTE reimbursement but at a fraction of the rate for credit-bearing courses.

2. *Reluctance to establish career programs for academic degree credit.* Despite the advantage of easy transfer between two- and four-year degree programs, states often have onerous and unwieldy approval procedures for credit classes, which are not responsive to evolving employer needs. Many faculty and administrators are also resistant to shifting the emphasis from the academic program to courses they consider less academically rigorous. For many professors, such a shift would also raise concerns about continued funding and career tenure, in itself a reflection of the strongly perceived separation between academic and vocational programs.

3. *Insufficient access and support policies.* State tuition and financial aid policies can make community college unaffordable for many students, especially part-time adult students. However, system regulations and policies often give little incentive for individual colleges to focus on the financial aid and support needs of disadvantaged students. In most states, adult education and ESL services are offered not in the community college but in the school district or other setting. These programs are not designed to prepare students for college-level work and rarely articulate into entry-level programs at college campuses. Even in states where community colleges are the main providers of these services, links to advanced certificate and degree-based career and vocational programs are weak at best. College system policies exacerbate the problem by limiting access for students who score below a basic skills threshold on a placement examination, relegating them to ABE and ESL divisions either off campus or within an entirely different division of the college. Colleges cannot serve all students with basic skills deficiencies, but they can serve many more than they currently do.

4. *Insufficient accountability measures and weak incentives.* Incentives and performance accountability can be a centerpiece of efforts to align college behavior with the career pathway vision. Unfortunately, performance systems rarely emphasize outcomes for the hardest to serve: students with low basic skills or from low-income communities. At one time, Florida's community college system focused on outcomes for disadvantaged students by offering bonus points for successful program completion and placement in a high-wage job. When the system recently eliminated the bonus for placement, few spoke out about how the change removed an important factor for encouraging schools to provide additional services for this population. Where performance measures do focus on the educationally and economically disadvantaged, the guidelines tend to come from outside the college system via WIA, the Carl D. Perkins Vocational and Technical Education Act, and other categorical programs and so are poorly aligned with the system's core measures. In several states, performance systems have been put in place with the idea that supplemental incentive funds beyond a college's base allocation could be used to foster new behavior and innovation. As state budgets

tighten, these supplemental funds have generally disappeared or become too small to effect significant change. Performance and funding is still driven by degree attainment indicators that are tied to the college's traditional academic transfer mission.

Where they now exist, career pathways will be strengthened with increased participation on the part of the institutional research function. Questions of accountability, access, and program outcome are best addressed by hard data. Because they are nimble, opportunistic, and fully engaged with the details of making their efforts bear fruit, new programs such as career pathways have not always forged a close connection with institutional research. Similarly, start-up career pathway programs could save considerable time in designing an evaluation framework by relying on institutional research. New and existing programs would benefit by access to institutional databases and the power they portend to benchmark career pathway outcomes. The attraction should be mutual. The innovation promised by career pathway programs coupled with the expertise inherent in institutional research can add transformative value to institutions.

References

Alssid, J., Gruber, D., Jenkins, D., Mazzeo, C., Roberts, B., and Stanback-Stroud, R. *Building a Career Pathways System: Promising Practices in Community College-Centered Workforce Development*. New York: Workforce Strategy Center, 2002.

Burton, L., and Celebuski, C. *Technical Education in 2-Year Colleges; HES 17*. Washington, D.C.: National Science Foundation, U.S. Dept. of Education, National Endowment for the Humanities, 1995.

Matus-Grossman, L., and Gooden, S. *Opening Doors: Students' Perspectives on Juggling Work, Family and College*. New York: MDRC, June 2002.

National Congress for Community Economic Development. "The Whole Agenda: The Past and Future of Community Development." In *Local Initiatives Support Corporation*. Washington, D.C.: National Congress for Community Economic Development, 2002.

JULIAN L. ALSSID *is executive director of the Workforce Strategy Center in Brooklyn, New York.*

DAVID GRUBER *is former director of the Workforce Strategy Center.*

DAVIS JENKINS, CHRISTOPHER MAZZEO, BRANDON ROBERTS, *and* REGINA STANBACK-STROUD *are senior consultants to the Workforce Strategy Center.*

8

This chapter describes techniques and projects that most institutions need if they are to be viable in an increasingly competitive labor market. The authors assert that institutional researchers who increase their involvement in workforce development initiatives can become more valuable to their institution.

An Action Agenda for Institutional Researchers

Lee Harvey, Richard A. Voorhees

With the growing focus on workforce development, it is an appropriate time for institutional research personnel to increase their involvement in instructional programming beyond the role required for program review and discontinuation. Many institutional researchers give substantial attention to analysis of institutional datasets that are often numerical in character. Employability and workforce development creates for institutional researchers a range of complex tasks and interesting conundrums. Employability and workforce development, with its highly qualitative (and to some extent situation-dependent) character, requires a particularly sophisticated analytical approach. This chapter outlines a series of undertakings implied by serious engagement with workforce development and employability.

There is a need to audit the institution to explore the extent to which employability development practices are embedded in programs, provided by central services (such as career advice and preparation), developed through extracurricular activity (linked or disengaged from institutional support), or missing altogether. Such an audit is a substantial undertaking. It requires systematic analysis, almost certainly relying on self-reporting (and supporting curriculum documentation) because the cost of face-to-face discussion with all program leaders would be prohibitive. It would, for example, be necessary to construct a pro forma to aid reporting of employability development, which is flexible enough to cater to all disciplines, years of study, and levels of qualification. This is no easy task, and institutional researchers should avoid the temptation to produce their own. Sharing practice here is vital. The audit needs to capture what happens in

NEW DIRECTIONS FOR INSTITUTIONAL RESEARCH, no. 128, Winter 2005 99 programs, down to the employability development on different modules; whether that development opportunity is formatively or summatively assessed; and whether it is integral to delivery of the subject matter, developed through peripheral activities, or reliant on some form of work experience or employer-linked project. The audit should identify whether the development activity is compulsory and thus affects all students on a program or voluntary, and if the latter then what proportion of them take up the opportunity. This, then, needs to be complemented by analysis of the take up of centrally provided employability development opportunities, such as those provided by career services, local employers, or student associations.

Institutional researchers can identify a baseline number of students from disadvantaged backgrounds in each discipline area. A penetration index could be calculated comparing historical enrollment by type of course or program pursued. This index would give institutional decision makers an overview of where opportunities lie. Again, this may involve some sophisticated analysis of available databases to identify "disadvantage."

Institutional researchers can help position their institution to effectively engage in workforce development, especially career pathways or widening participation, by identifying baseline data on the number of disadvantaged adults that they might serve from their region. Census data can be helpful in pinpointing the areas within the college's traditional service area where demographics indicate a potential demand for career pathway services.

Along with institutional auditing, student surveys toward the end of their program can gather their perception of the program's effectiveness in enhancing their employability. An employability experience questionnaire, for example, is being developed in conjunction with the Higher Education Academy in the UK. Many of the student satisfaction surveys developed initially at the Centre for Research into Quality at the University of Central England in the UK include suites of questions about skill and attribute development, student satisfaction with placement and internship, as well as links with industry.

A major challenge for institutional researchers, in conjunction with program leaders, is to develop methods through which the complexities of employability might be picked up in assessment practices. Despite considerable advances in fostering explicit employability development opportunities, little evident advance has been made on the modes of assessing a range of employability and workforce development attributes. Apart from the standard written assignment tasks, most students engage in few skill-assessment activities other than group projects or oral presentations. Institutional researchers could develop and pilot imaginative approaches to assessing a range of attributes, from risk taking to leadership.

Working with program leaders and software developers, institutional researchers could help identify the elements necessary for recording students' attainment and aid in designing student-friendly self-reflection tools. In the UK, for example, initiation of "personal development programming"

(PDP), which combines career management with reflection on experience of academic and extracurricular activity, is under way; there is an opportunity for institutional researchers to aid that innovative process but also to evaluate its impact and effectiveness. This would involve analyzing the content of personal development files (PDFs) and exploring with students and teachers the function, value, and utility of the files. It might further lead to researching how employers relate to PDFs and the use they make of them in the recruitment processes.

Widespread engagement of institutions with alumni offers the prospect of surveys designed to follow up the extent to which a program's attention to employability is coherent with alumni experiences in the world of work. This would be an important task to see if there is any correlation between how a program aims to develop employability and the attributes students require when first recruited and then after a period of years.

A trickier but no less important and rewarding task for institutional researchers would be to research the relationship between student employment (attained level, activities undertaken) and the range of employability enhancement activities the student engages in while on the program of study. This would probably involve a cohort tracking study and fairly in-depth periodic interviewing to explore perception, attainment, and intention at various stages. A natural supplement to this would be to explore the extent to which student performance in assessed aspects of employability attributes in the program reflected their actual employment or perception of how well they were prepared for employment by their program of study.

Institutional researchers have a role in aligning programs by focusing on employers and employment needs, using a variety of techniques as outlined by Voorhees in Chapter Three. There probably is no better place within a given institution to centralize external information about job markets and competitor programs than the institutional research office.

A key role for institutional researchers in exploring employer needs is to conduct employer surveys. These have other benefits; they also promote employer involvement in program development. Employer surveys are extremely useful, but the data are often hard to obtain. Experience suggests that employer surveys result in a low response rate and generate skewed datasets, with uneven responses depending on the type of institution. Face-to-face inquiry fares much better than a postal survey but is much more expensive and time-consuming. Furthermore, there is a tendency to think that an "employer" has a single view. This is not the case, as the Graduates' Work study showed (Harvey, Burrows, and Green, 1992). The line manager of a graduate recruit, the graduate recruitment office, and the senior managers often had quite divergent perspectives on what constituted a good graduate.

A proxy for direct exploration of employer requirements is to survey current students, especially part-timers. Surveys of current students can produce invaluable insights for assessing market potentials. Although current students tend to be oversurveyed, information an institution might collect selectively from surveys of current students would include preferences for scheduling options, delivery mechanisms, perception of existing college services, and preference for specific programs.

Institutional researchers could also examine new target markets. As institutions expand into new markets, the preferences of prospective students for scheduling, program content, and institutional services need to match the institution's ability to deliver. The use of the VALS typology (Chapter Three) may augment more traditional market research. The emerging field of psychographic market research can certainly yield new insights for targeted geographical areas in which the institution may consider program expansion.

Institutional researchers have a role in augmenting and monitoring new programs. Working with student recruiters, curriculum modifiers and deliverers, and student services during the initiation and preimplementation phases of program development, institutional researchers can be active in refining programs at the early stages and evaluating the success of new programs once they are up and running.

Another area of research would be to explore the nature of employers' recruitment processes. Do they, for example, systematically seek out and evaluate specific skills? How idiosyncratic are their recruitment desires and practices? Does this vary from discipline to discipline? To what extent do employers link recruitment to subject studied? This information will be useful for students, lecturing staff, and program designers. In many instances, academics in higher education and their students have little idea of the mechanisms and criteria by which employers select students through recruitment processes. This is not to suggest that academics must be steered in what they teach by employers' recruitment methods; far from it, given the bizarre nature of some recruitment. However, it is better not to be ignorant of the link between higher education and employment.

The data derived from employers can give staff developers and academics a set of information to help them devise a series of practices to enhance student employability. These might be assistance for students to more quickly gain employment on the basis of evaluation of employer recruitment techniques, such as curriculum vitae writing, interviewing techniques, and coping with assessment centers, on through to more fundamental practices such as developing a range of communication skills, teaching students to work in teams through development of various roles, and offering a range of real-world problem-solving activities. The employer-focused research undertaken by institutional researchers would lend guidance on the specific construction of these enhancement activities.

A key task for institutional researchers linked to workforce development would be to help guide strategy. Armed with an array of employability information, institutional researchers could work with staff developers, central service providers, and senior managers in institutions to inform a strategy that is the basis of a generic guide to program leaders and central service providers.

Workforce development programs are not inexpensive to operate. Institutional researchers should familiarize themselves with the range of external financial support available to students and programs. For example, in the United States clarity about Pell Grant eligibility, WIA individual training accounts, and other resources that are available in state or foundation scholarship programs can answer basic questions about the feasibility of starting new institutional efforts. These input resources can be paired with knowledge of current program cost, especially for remedial programs, so that institutions can more effectively engage external funders in dialogue about what it costs to educate disadvantaged adults.

It is often onerous for institutions to create and maintain accountability systems for workforce programs such as WIA and Perkins (see Chapter Five). Institutional researchers carry much of the accountability burden when their institution chooses to participate in these programs and as a result requires familiarization with tracking systems that are both internal and external to the institution.

Although there are important reasons to report these data to external audiences, institutional researchers should analyze them internally because they will want to engage in cohort tracking of disadvantaged adults to determine where best institutional practices lie in promoting their success. This requires interinstitutional cooperation to identify disadvantaged adults when they enroll and the technical expertise to track their attendance across one or more semesters. Careful analysis of their experiences within an institution illuminates which internal pathways can be modified to meet institutional expectations to deliver a quality program.

Workforce development and employability offers an extensive array of potential new areas of activity for institutional researchers. These seem to be exciting prospects, moving the institutional researcher role closer to policy and strategy.

Reference

Harvey, L., Burrows, A. and Green, D. *Someone Who Can Make an Impression. Report of the Employers' Survey of Qualities of Higher Education Graduates.* Birmingham, England: QHE, 1992.

LEE HARVEY is professor and director of the Centre for Research and Evaluation at Sheffield Hallam University, United Kingdom.

RICHARD A. VOORHEES is principal of Voorhees Group LLC, an independent higher education consulting company in Littleton, Colorado.

INDEX

Ward, R., 23
Wenger, E., 48
Williams, G., 54
Williams, J., 18
Wilson, R., 21
Wingrove, J., 42
Winn, S., 21
Women, 33
Work experience: ad hoc options for, 21–22; employers' view of, 19–20; external variation of, 21; forms of, 20–22; influence of, in recruitment, 51–52; learning from, 22; of mature students, 44–45; as part of a program of study, 20
Work shadowing, 20

Workforce: future requirements of, 8; higher education's importance to, 8; number of workers in, 10; shortage of, 7–8
Workforce agencies, 93
Workforce Investment Act (WIA; 1998): accountability provisions of, 61–67; maintenance of, 60–61; overview of, 11
Workforce investment boards (WIBs), 60, 64
Workforce Strategy Center, 84, 85
Workplace literacy programs, 88
Wyber, J., 14

Yorke, M., 2, 20, 41, 48, 50, 53, 54

Back Issue/Subscription Order Form

Copy or detach and send to:

Jossey-Bass, A Wiley Imprint, 989 Market Street, San Francisco CA 94103-1741

Call or fax toll-free: Phone 888-378-2537 6:30AM – 3PM PST; Fax 888-481-2665

Back Issues: Please send me the following issues at $29 each

(Important: please include ISBN number for each issue.)

_____

_____

_____

$ _____   Total for single issues

$ _____   SHIPPING CHARGES: SURFACE   Domestic Canadian

| | | First Item | $5.00 | $6.00 |
| | | Each Add'l Item | $3.00 | $1.50 |

For next-day and second-day delivery rates, call the number listed above.

Subscriptions   Please __ start __ renew my subscription to *New Directions for Institutional Research* for the year 2_____at the following rate:

U.S.   __ Individual $80   __ Institutional $170

Canada   __ Individual $80   __ Institutional $210

All Others   __ Individual $104   __ Institutional $244

Online subscriptions are available via Wiley InterScience!

**For more information about online subscriptions visit
www.wileyinterscience.com**

$ _____   Total single issues and subscriptions (Add appropriate sales tax for your state for single issue orders. No sales tax for U.S. subscriptions. Canadian residents, add GST for subscriptions and single issues.)

__Payment enclosed (U.S. check or money order only)

__VISA __ MC __ AmEx # _____ Exp. Date _____

Signature _____ Day Phone _____

__ Bill Me (U.S. institutional orders only. Purchase order required.)

Purchase order # _____
          Federal Tax ID13559302   **GST 89102 8052**

Name _____

Address _____

_____

Phone _____ E-mail _____

For more information about Jossey-Bass, visit our Web site at www.josseybass.com

IR122   **Assessing Character Outcomes in College**
Jon C. Dalton, Terrence R. Russell, Sally Kline
Examines several perspectives on the role of higher education in developing
students' character, and illustrates approaches to defining and assessing
character outcomes. Moral, civic, ethical, and spiritual development are key
aspects of students' growth and experience in college, so how can educators
encourage good values and assess their impact?
ISBN: 0-7879-7791-8

IR121   **Overcoming Survey Research Problems**
Stephen R. Porter
As demand for survey research has increased, survey response rates have
decreased. This volume examines an array of survey research problems and
best practices, from both the literature and field practitioners, to provide
solutions to increase response rates while controlling costs. Discusses
administering longitudinal studies, doing surveys on sensitive topics such as
student drug and alcohol use, and using new technologies for survey
administration.
ISBN: 0-7879-7477-3

IR120   **Using Geographic Information Systems in Institutional Research**
Daniel Teodorescu
Exploring the potential of geographic information systems (GIS) applications in
higher education administration, this issue introduces IR professionals and
campus administrators to a powerful presentation and analysis tool. Chapters
explore the benefits of working with the spatial component of data in
recruitment, admissions, facilities, alumni development, and other areas, with
examples of actual GIS applications from several higher education institutions.
ISBN: 0-7879-7281-9

IR119   **Maximizing Revenue in Higher Education**
F. King Alexander, Ronald G. Ehrenberg
This volume presents edited versions of some of the best articles from a forum
on institutional revenue generation sponsored by the Cornell Higher Education
Research Institute. The chapters provide different perspectives on revenue
generation and how institutions are struggling to find an appropriate balance
between meeting public expectations and maximizing private market forces.
The insights provided about options and alternatives will enable campus
leaders, institutional researchers, and policymakers to better understand
evolving patterns in public and private revenue reliance.
ISBN: 0-7879-7221-5

IR118   **Studying Diverse Institutions: Contexts, Challenges, and Considerations**
M. Christopher Brown II, Jason E. Lane
This volume examines the contextual and methodological issues pertaining to
studying diverse institutions (including women's colleges, tribal colleges, and
military academies), and provides effective and useful approaches for higher
education administrators, institutional researchers and planners, policymakers,
and faculty seeking to better understand students in postsecondary education.
It also offers guidelines to asking the right research questions, employing the
appropriate research design and methods, and analyzing the data with respect
to the unique institutional contexts.
ISBN: 0-7879-6990-7

IR117   **Unresolved Issues in Conducting Salary-Equity Studies**
Robert K. Toutkoushian
Chapters discuss the issues surrounding how to use faculty rank, seniority, and
experience as control variables in salary-equity studies. Contributors review the

challenges of conducting a salary-equity study for nonfaculty administrators and staff—who constitute the majority of employees, even in academic institutions—and examine the advantages and disadvantages of using hierarchical linear modeling to measure pay equity. They present a case-study approach to illustrate the political and practical challenges that researchers often face when conducting a salary-equity study for an institution. This is a companion volume to Conducting Salary-Equity Studies: Alternative Approaches to Research (IR115).
ISBN: 0-7879-6863-3

IR116   **Reporting Higher Education Results: Missing Links in the Performance Chain**
Joseph C. Burke, Henrick P. Minassians
The authors review performance reporting's coverage, content, and customers, they examine in depth the reporting indicators, types, and policy concerns, and they compare them among different states' reports. They highlight weaknesses in our current performance reporting—such as a lack of comparable indicators for assessing the quality of undergraduate education—and make recommendations about how to best use and improve performance information.
ISBN: 0-7879-6336-4

IR115   **Conducting Salary-Equity Studies: Alternative Approaches to Research**
Robert K. Toutkoushian
Synthesizing nearly 30 years of research on salary equity from the field of economics and the experiences of past studies, this issue launches an important dialogue between scholars and institutional researchers on the methodology and application of salary-equity studies in today's higher education institutions. The first of a two-volume set on the subject, it also bridges the gap between academic research and the more pragmatic statistical and political considerations in real-life institutional salary studies.
ISBN: 0-7879-6335-6

IR114   **Evaluating Faculty Performance**
Carol L. Colbeck
This issue brings new insights to faculty work and its assessment in light of reconsideration of faculty work roles, rapid technological change, increasing bureaucratization of the core work of higher education, and public accountability for performance. Exploring successful methods that individuals, institutions, and promotion and tenure committees are using for evaluations of faculty performance for career development, this issue is an indispensable guide to academic administrators and institutional researchers involved in the faculty evaluation process.
ISBN: 0-7879-6334-8

IR113   **Knowledge Management: Building a Competitive Advantage in Higher Education**
Andreea M. Serban, Jing Luan
Provides a comprehensive discussion of knowledge management, covering its theoretical, practical, and technological aspects with an emphasis on their relevance for applications in institutional research. Chapters examine the theoretical basis and impact of data mining; discuss the role of institutional research in customer relationship management; and provide a framework for the integration of institutional research within the larger context of organization learning. With a synopsis of technologies that support knowledge management and an exploration of future developments in this field, this volume assists

institutional researchers and analysts in taking advantage of the opportunities of knowledge management and addressing its challenges.
ISBN: 0-7879-6291-0

IR112   **Balancing Qualitative and Quantitative Information for Effective Decision Support**
Richard D. Howard, Kenneth W. Borland Jr.
Establishes methods for integration of numeric data and its contextual application. With theoretical and practical examples, contributors explore the techniques and realities of creating, communicating, and using balanced decision support information. Chapters discuss the critical role of measurement in building institutional quality; examples of conceptual and theoretical frameworks and their application for the creation of evaluation information; and methods of communicating data and information in relation to its decision support function.
ISBN: 0-7879-5796-8

IR111   **Higher Education as Competitive Enterprise: When Markets Matter**
Robert Zemsky, Susan Shaman, Daniel B. Shapiro
Offers a comprehensive history of the development and implementation of Collegiate Results Instrument (CRI), a tool for mapping the connection between market forces and educational outcomes in higher education. Chapters detail the methods that CRI uses to help institutions to remain value centered by becoming market smart.
ISBN: 0-7879-5795-X

IR110   **Measuring What Matters: Competency-Based Learning Models in Higher Education**
Richard Voorhees
An analysis of the findings of the National Postsecondary Education Cooperative project on data and policy implications of national skill standards, this issue provides researchers, faculty, and academic administrators with the tools needed to deal effectively with the emerging competency-based initiatives.
ISBN: 0-7879-1411-8

IR109   **The Student Ratings Debate: Are They Valid? How Can We Best Use Them?**
Michael Theall, Philip C. Abrami, Lisa A. Mets
Presents a thorough analysis of the use of student evaluations of teaching for summative decisions and discusses the ongoing controversies, emerging research, and dissenting opinions on their utility and validity. Summarizes the role of student ratings as tools for instructional improvement, as evidence for promotion and tenure decisions, as the means for student course selection, as a criterion of program effectiveness, and as the continuing focus of active research and intensive discussion.
ISBN: 0-7879-5756-9

IR108   **Collaboration Between Student Affairs and Institutional Researchers to Improve Institutional Effectiveness**
J. Worth Pickering, Gary R. Hanson
Defines the unique aspects of student affairs research, including its role in responding to assessment mandates and accreditation agencies, its use of student development theory in formulating research questions, the value of qualitative methods it employs, and the potential contribution it can make to institutional decision making.
ISBN: 0-7879-5727-5

United States Postal Service

Statement of Ownership, Management, and Circulation

1. Publication Title	2. Publication Number	3. Filing Date
New Directions For Institutional Research	0 2 7 1 - 0 5 7 9	10/1/05

4. Issue Frequency	5. Number of Issues Published Annually	6. Annual Subscription Price
Quarterly	4	$170.00

7. Complete Mailing Address of Known Office of Publication (Not printer) (Street, city, county, state, and ZIP+4)

Wiley Subscription Services, Inc. at Jossey-Bass, 989 Market Street, San Francisco, CA 94103

Contact Person
Joe Schuman
Telephone
(415) 782-3232

8. Complete Mailing Address of Headquarters or General Business Office of Publisher (Not printer)

Wiley Subscription Services, Inc. 111 River Street, Hoboken, NJ 07030

9. Full Names and Complete Mailing Addresses of Publisher, Editor, and Managing Editor (Do not leave blank)

Publisher (Name and complete mailing address)

Wiley, San Francisco, 989 Market Street, San Francisco, CA 94103-1741

Editor (Name and complete mailing address)

Robert Toutkoushian, WW Wright Educ. Bldg Rm 4220, IN. Univ. School of Educ. 201 N. Rose Ave. Bloomington, IN 47405

Managing Editor (Name and complete mailing address)

None

10. Owner (Do not leave blank. If the publication is owned by a corporation, give the name and address of the corporation immediately followed by the names and addresses of all stockholders owning or holding 1 percent or more of the total amount of stock. If not owned by a corporation, give the names and addresses of the individual owners. If owned by a partnership or other unincorporated firm, give its name and address as well as those of each individual owner. If the publication is published by a nonprofit organization, give its name and address.)

Full Name	Complete Mailing Address
Wiley Subscription Services, Inc.	111 River Street, Hoboken, NJ 07030
(see attached list)	

11. Known Bondholders, Mortgagees, and Other Security Holders Owning or Holding 1 Percent or More of Total Amount of Bonds, Mortgages, or Other Securities. If none, check box ☑ None

Full Name	Complete Mailing Address
None	None

12. Tax Status (For completion by nonprofit organizations authorized to mail at nonprofit rates) (Check one)
The purpose, function, and nonprofit status of this organization and the exempt status for federal income tax purposes:
☐ Has Not Changed During Preceding 12 Months
☐ Has Changed During Preceding 12 Months (Publisher must submit explanation of change with this statement)

PS Form 3526, October 1999   (See Instructions on Reverse)

---

13. Publication Title	14. Issue Date for Circulation Data Below
New Directions For Institutional Research	Spring 2005

15.	Extent and Nature of Circulation		Average No. Copies Each Issue During Preceding 12 Months	No. Copies of Single Issue Published Nearest to Filing Date
a.	Total Number of Copies (Net press run)		1912	1854
b. Paid and/or Requested Circulation	(1)	Paid/Requested Outside-County Mail Subscriptions Stated on Form 3541. (Include advertiser's proof and exchange copies)	680	675
	(2)	Paid In-County Subscriptions Stated on Form 3541 (Include advertiser's proof and exchange copies)	0	0
	(3)	Sales Through Dealers and Carriers, Street Vendors, Counter Sales, and Other Non-USPS Paid Distribution	0	0
	(4)	Other Classes Mailed Through the USPS	0	0
c.	Total Paid and/or Requested Circulation (Sum of 15b. (1), (2),(3),and (4)) ▲		680	675
d. Free Distribution by Mail (Samples, compliment-ary, and other free)	(1)	Outside-County as Stated on Form 3541	0	0
	(2)	In-County as Stated on Form 3541	0	0
	(3)	Other Classes Mailed Through the USPS	0	0
e.	Free Distribution Outside the Mail (Carriers or other means)		52	51
f.	Total Free Distribution (Sum of 15d. and 15e.) ▲		52	51
g.	Total Distribution (Sum of 15c. and 15f) ▲		743	726
h.	Copies not Distributed		1169	1128
i.	Total (Sum of 15g. and h.) ▲		1912	1854
j.	Percent Paid and/or Requested Circulation (15c. divided by 15g. times 100)		93%	93%

16. Publication of Statement of Ownership
☑ Publication required. Will be printed in the Winter 2005 issue of this publication. ☐ Publication not required.

17. Signature and Title of Editor, Publisher, Business Manager, or Owner

Susan E. Lewis, VP & Publisher - Periodicals

Date 10/01/05

I certify that all information furnished on this form is true and complete. I understand that anyone who furnishes false or misleading information on this form or who omits material or information requested on the form may be subject to criminal sanctions (including fines and imprisonment) and/or civil sanctions (including civil penalties).

Instructions to Publishers

1. Complete and file one copy of this form with your postmaster annually on or before October 1. Keep a copy of the completed form for your records.

2. In cases where the stockholder or security holder is a trustee, include in items 10 and 11 the name of the person or corporation for whom the trustee is acting. Also include the names and addresses of individuals who own or hold 1 percent or more of the total amount of bonds, mortgages, or other securities of the publishing corporation. In item 11, if none, check the box. Use blank sheets if more space is required.

3. Be sure to furnish all circulation information called for in item 15. Free circulation must be shown in items 15d, e, and f.

4. Item 15h., Copies not Distributed, must include (1) newsstand copies originally stated on Form 3541, and returned to the publisher, (2) estimated returns from news agents, and (3), copies for office use, leftovers, spoiled, and all other copies not distributed.

5. If the publication had Periodicals authorization as a general or requester publication, this Statement of Ownership, Management, and Circulation must be published; it must be printed in any issue in October, if the publication is not published during October, the first issue printed after October.

6. In item 16, indicate the date of the issue in which this Statement of Ownership will be published.

7. Item 17 must be signed.

Failure to file or publish a statement of ownership may lead to suspension of Periodicals authorization.

PS Form **3526**, October 1999 (Reverse)

WITHDRAWAL